You can't see th

Japanese saying

SELLING DOG FOOD IN JAPAN

Barbara Hauser

BOOK FOUR

ISBN 978-0-9706026-0-2

Published by Mesatop Press

Minnesota, USA

Dedicated to my parents, who passed on a love of travel.

And to my husband, Doug, my favorite traveling companion.

Not all those who wander are lost.

J.R.R. Tolkein

contents

Life is either a daring
adventure or nothing.

HELEN KELLER

chapter one

SELLING DOG FOOD IN JAPAN

"YOU WILL NEVER SUCCEED, BARBARA."

He said this to me like it was a piece of information he was nice enough to take his time and trouble to hand to me. Superior in height and authority, he looked down at me as we stood in his office doorway. He could not have been more patronizing. I was speechless. There was a lot I thought of saying, but he was the managing partner of our law firm.

I had stopped by to get his "permission" for a new exciting project I had organized. I had been looking forward to showing him what I had put together. What was my special project? It was linked to one of my clients who distributed a premium label dog food.

I didn't even have a dog. But I did have an elegant corner office in a Minneapolis law firm, and in the 1980s I was one of the few women lawyers to become a partner in a major law firm anywhere in the United States. Many of my colleagues, male and female, seemed quite content to coast on for the rest of their working lives. My problem was that I was getting a bit bored. Most of my work was with entrepreneurs. I'd do their estate planning—my technical expertise—and also their general corporate work. All of the work was in Minnesota though.

I had always wanted to practice international law. Then I could combine my legal knowledge and my love of travel—a perfect combination. As I analyzed my situation I couldn't see much hope of any international work: all of our clients were in U.S. businesses. Maybe I could come up with a plan to do some international work? To start with, where in the world should I focus?

One day at home, when our three children were at day care and kindergarten, I got out a stack of atlases and maps and spread them over our large dining table, puzzling about where in the world I should try to do something. I remember that the woman who cleaned our house was curious and asked what I was doing. I tried explaining. She said, "I'm glad I don't have to do that." And I was glad I didn't have to clean our house.

There I was, wondering where in the world I would like to do some legal work. It was in the late 1980s. Europe was excited about forming and expanding the European Union—but I was skeptical of the lasting success of pooling together such different cultures. I didn't think it would last.

If I was going to explore the whole world I thought, "Why not try something really hard while I am at it? Maybe Japan?" It was a heady time for Japan. Their economy was booming, thanks to the "bubble" that had not yet burst. The Japanese consumers had money to burn—and they coveted American brands.

We had spent a wonderful family vacation in Japan a few years earlier. For that trip I had studied several books of manners and customs in Japan. The six of us—my husband, three sons and one school friend of a son who claimed to know Japanese—had train passes, and we spent three weeks on our own in the countryside of Japan, where we encountered pervasive helpfulness, mixed with occasional giggles at us.

For our part, we seemed full of clumsy errors—we couldn't even order two bottles of beer. We'd be served three or four but never two. I learned later that, unbelievably, there are different sets of counting words depending on the type and/or shape of what is being counted! Definitely a difficult country for me to master. I liked challenges.

With these thoughts rumbling around in the back of my mind, one late afternoon I answered my office phone just as I was planning to leave to get home early during the Christmas holidays. The office was quiet; nearly everyone had left. My dog food client was on the phone. He was calling to thank me for sending a poinsettia to wish him a Merry Christmas. I decided to chat with him for a few minutes and asked what was new, how his business was going, etc. "Well," he told me, "I was just at a trade show in Chicago and a group of Japanese men wanted a lot of information about our premium, all natural, brand dog food."

He made this as an idle passing comment and was ready to move on, wish me a Merry Christmas, and end the conversation. I heard the word "Japan," though, and wanted to stop and visit this idea.

Without much thought, I told him I was thinking of going to Japan anyway for other reasons—a bit of a stretch at that time! Would he like me to follow up with the Japanese men who were interested in his dog food? My thinking was that if I could get a few of my law firm clients to do business in Japan, then I could help them with their international legal work. Details to follow.

With dog food "signed up" during the next week, I called some other clients. One was a high-end blanket weaving company—wouldn't their soft blankets be a success in Japan? I thought the quality and handcrafted look would be appealing in Japan. Another client made helium balloons. Yet another made decorated socks! I called all the retail product clients I could think of. I was nervous, but I had my pitch down: "I will be going to Japan anyway, with another partner. While I am there, would you like me to see if there's an interest in your product?" All at no charge to them. All except the helium balloon maker said, "Sure."

By then I did in fact have a "partner"—whom I'll call Linda. I met Linda at the International Center in Minneapolis. She had been a flight attendant and was looking for new work. "Well, well," I thought. "As a flight attendant she had covered the Japan route. She had been in Tokyo many times. She could help me navigate the cryptic subway system. Her husband worked for an international company and had some contacts in Tokyo; he could make some introductions for us."

So I asked Linda if she'd like to come with me to Tokyo—all at my expense—and we could see if there was an interest in any of my clients' products. I would also be glad to have company on this risky adventure.

In my free time, I formed a new company "International Access, Inc.," complete with letterhead and business cards. The name on the card was printed in gold! The "access" referred to helping clients gain access to other markets in other country.

At that time, our Minnesota clients didn't know how to expand into other countries. One client, for example, asked me what he needed to put on clothing labels if he wanted to try selling his clothing in "Europe." He actually wasn't sure which countries he had in mind and had never been in any of them. I liked the idea of helping them gain "access" to new markets.

Next on my new project list, I had to get "approval" from our law firm's managing partner to be gone for two weeks on a Japan trip. I briefly explained the purpose of my trip.

He interrupted with, "You will never succeed, Barbara." He knew this, he explained, because "Ed and I went to Tokyo once for a client. We presented a deal to them and told them we needed to have their response the next day. They said they weren't ready yet, and we never heard from them again." He threw in, "Besides they don't work with women."

Finally he got intrigued by my plan. He informed me, in another nugget of wisdom: "All the profits you make belong to the law firm."

I countered that the law firm would then have to pay my trip expenses, some $12,000.

He quickly changed to, "This is your personal project," and wished me luck.

I shared my doubts with our supportive law firm marketing manager, wondering if I could really do this. She asked what would be the worst that could happen.

My reply was, "They could laugh." She laughed hard at that, and I was ready to go.

My new partner and I were off. Northwest Airlines nonstop to Tokyo. I wanted to keep our image consistent with the gold printing on our business cards, so we went first class all the way. On Northwest we were in the small upper deck, about ten seats total with great dedicated service. During boarding the speakers played Vivaldi's Four Seasons; our personal cabin attendant passed out champagne before takeoff. Very nice.

I already knew about the Japanese fascination with designer brands. I wanted to make a very good impression. I gulped at the price but had bought a Louis Vuitton briefcase—$1,000! I packed my genuine Chanel jewelry. From our family trip I had learned how curious many of the Japanese were about our family. I brought along a booklet of photos of my family and my house, something I never would have done on a regular business trip.

In Tokyo I had booked two rooms at the Imperial Palace. The hotel staff stood next to the elevators, in their traditional uniforms, to bow at each arriving and departing passenger. The lobby was enormous. First item of business was to have the hotel business center print more business cards with Japanese on one side. We were set to go.

Where to start? We went to the World Trade Center with our samples. We didn't get very far there. They seem perplexed by us, and we didn't actually sound very certain of what we were doing. But we kept going. We got in touch with one of Linda's husband's contacts. He did arrange some meetings. I remember one in particular. We had about twelve people around a round table that rotated, filled with dishes of Chinese food. We passed around the socks during dinner. How strange we must have seemed, and how polite they were. But they had no interest in socks.

I had gotten the names of the Japanese men who were interested in my client's dog food. That meeting was a hit. They turned out to be the top management of the prestigious Japan Kennel Club. They liked that our dog food was American, had all natural ingredients, and especially that it was very expensive. They wanted to have "the best." They also wanted an exclusive distributorship. Aha, that would be a legal agreement!

This was the beginning of a fascinating, slow, and steady two-year relationship with the Japan Kennel Club. My dog food client had never been to Japan. In fact he had never had a passport. So I would be his cultural and travel guide. He didn't seem to find it confusing that I would be switching roles as we progressed.

I started with the International Access card, including Linda at the beginning, until the project switched to an entirely legal one, and it turned out that she wanted to spend time working on some house construction issues at her home. I continued my trips to Tokyo on my own and had a number of meetings with the Japan Kennel Club. As soon as it looked like it was turning into pure legal work I got out my law firm card. Those expenses and profits were now for the law firm.

I had a great time. I kept studying Japanese manners and customs. I enjoyed the slow way business was done. I learned that they never said "no"—but the meaning was clear from "that would be difficult," said with nearly closed lips. Everyone liked looking at my family photos. In all the meetings and meals with my clients, I never met a single wife. One of the men did take his daughter and me on a car trip to some famous temples for an overnight stay. We were supposed to be at a hot springs resort with a good view of Mount Fuji. It was cloudy the whole time—no hot springs and no Mount Fuji.

We were using faxes at that time, the kind where the paper curled and faded. I remember beginning each fax to Japan with some statement about the weather or trees or flowers, then asking after someone's health, and finally getting to the point of the fax. I learned how important it was to acknowledge receipt of the fax immediately, even if the actual responses would come later. This is a habit that carries over today to acknowledging receipt of emails.

About dogs—what did I learn? Apparently Japanese dogs are special. They have special taste preferences. This fact was repeated to me many times, very solemnly. One day I actually spent several hours in a stuffy conference room, complete with an English interpreter and ten men from the Kennel Club, staring at the latest taste test results, in Japanese of course, which were passed around and soberly commented on. This was a great, refreshing change from sitting in my corner office in Minnesota. I even went to two all-day Japanese dog shows.

About working with Japanese men—what did I learn? Relationships are the center of business. No one ever mentioned that I was a woman. When we did get to the legal agreement, I presented a standard six-page section on detailed dispute resolution. We all knew each other fairly well by then. They said "no" nicely and what went in the final agreement was a section that would horrify my law firm partners: "If there is a disagreement, the parties agree to discuss it."

Agreements were signed and all went well for a long time. Then an impatient American bought the dog food company and my mild-mannered, polite client was no longer in charge. The new owner's attitude caused the Japanese to turn to me for help. They faxed me about all their problems. The container ships weren't loaded neatly enough. They were busy faxing me. There was one problem after another. I tried to keep helping, but the new owner told me, "Never mind; I don't need your help. I can take care of everything myself." So the frustrated Japanese men were told to quit faxing me. I assume the arrangement fell apart.

I got to keep some great memories and lessons. I had never thought I would be selling dog food in Japan. I still didn't have a dog. What else might I end up doing?

This *Daruma* is used in Japan for new projects: you paint in the left eye when you begin and the right eye when you have finished. I have a large collection of them!

chapter two

THE SWISS TAX TREATY

ONE UNFORGETTABLE LEGAL PROJECT PITTED ME, all by myself, in a challenge to the formidable, respected Swiss tax authorities. As the most senior female law firm partner, I had been adding into my practice more and more complex matters to untangle. The cross-border estate tax treaty agreements are some of the most complicated legal agreements I've ever seen. I enjoyed trying to figure them out.

My knowledge was self-taught. No one else in the firm understood the treaties—indeed only a few lawyers in New York had ever worked with estate tax treaties. All of the attention about treaties was spent on the many income tax treaties. Estate tax treaties are rare, and seldom read. How had I gotten involved with the treaties?

Most of my estate planning clients had been predictable. I knew what plans they would need, and I had become well-versed in the tax laws that applied to them. My main focus had been on the U.S. estate tax. I knew it so well that I was a frequent lecturer to groups of other lawyers. I also wrote a number of articles. I was on a statewide drafting committee. It was all getting very routine. For me that meant it would soon be boring—not a situation I liked at all.

One day in 1990 this changed. One of my litigation partners buzzed me on the intercom phone: "Barbara, can you come over right now and meet a client who needs a will?"

His client had just won a lawsuit settlement in the millions and had no will.

I went over to his office, was introduced to the client, and started asking him my routine questions. Note: Identifying characteristics have been changed.

My questions were basically "What do you own? Where is it? What is its value?" When I got to questions about where the assets were—the answers were very different from my usual client interviews. In addition to the new settlement award, he owned a flat in London that was itself owned by a company in the Isle of Jersey. I had never heard of that and wasn't too sure where that island was.

He went on. He also owned one-half of an apartment in the best part of Paris. I did know exactly where that was: the 16th *arrondisement*. Continuing with the list, he told me he owned a villa outside of Rome. He owned some collections of silver and jewelry stored in bank vaults in Switzerland. He was a U.S. citizen and a legal resident of Switzerland. Wow! Where would I start?

Finally I had some legal work that combined my international interests with my legal expertise. However—and this was a fairly big hurdle—I didn't actually know what to do about any of this.

I had questions about each of the "foreign" assets. What law would apply? How would I find out? Should I find a lawyer who already knew these issues and could take care of it or could help me? Should I just refer the whole matter to a lawyer who knew more? I did not like that idea. I finally had some fascinating international legal work assigned to me as a law firm matter. I wanted to figure this out myself.

I started by calling the local offices of some of the "big six" accounting firms in the countries where the assets were. I quickly learned that the foreign offices had lawyers and accountants who were focused only on corporate transactions. They had no knowledge of, or interest in, private client estate planning. They did not even have any suggestions for me.

Next I tried calling some highly qualified lawyers in those countries. I learned a lot from all the calls, trying to find someone who could help, but I couldn't find anyone or anything that could help me.

I did learn that "estate planning" was not a very developed field in European countries. In the legal profession it was not even the "lawyers" who usually worked with inheritance, wills, and related tax issues; it was the *notaires* and they seemed to do less "planning" than in the United States. Because the client was a U.S. citizen I did know that the full U.S. estate tax would apply to all of his assets. So the U.S. part, which I was so familiar with, was not a problem. The problem was figuring out how all those other countries would treat his assets. I had no idea at all.

I sat over at my round client table one day, wondering, "What shall I do?" I needed to have a plan. It wouldn't be fair to the client to not understand the foreign assets he owned. In fact, there was no urgency for the client since he was alive and well. The urgency would come whenever the client might die. Meanwhile I could do his regular U.S. estate and tax planning.

I'm the one who felt some urgency, even if it was mainly an intellectual urgency. I was intrigued by the eventual puzzles and wanted to know how to deal with them. But I hadn't found any lawyer who seemed to know a lot about these international issues. I felt stuck.

Suddenly I had an inspiration. I called the dean of the University of Minnesota Law School: "How would you like me to teach a seminar on international estate planning?"

I had known him for years and had taught Supreme Court seminars as a part-time activity for several years. He didn't hesitate—but his answer wasn't quite what I expected: "Sure," he said, "and you could also teach federal income tax."

So we had a deal. The seminar would be for fifteen weeks. I thought that should be enough time for me to organize the subject and figure out what I thought I should know—i.e., what I would be teaching my students each week.

We made it through, the students and I, with me one week ahead of the students. When the seminar ended, I boxed up the course materials I had put together—including copies of the estate tax treaties, which had been hard to find—and sent them to the national legal course books publisher. A few weeks later my box came back, with a note: "Thank you very much, but we do not think there would be much interest in this subject."

Anyway that client and that seminar gave me a good start in international estate planning. I ended up being the founder of the International Estate Planning Commission in the Union Internationale des Avocats, and in 2000 I sat down and wrote a full legal treatise on international estate planning, which I still update each summer. I did not have any assistants. I wrote each word and I read each case and each tax code provision. If I made any mistakes they would be mine. I did read the few other books in the field, but I did not use them as references. I went directly to the language of the codes and treaties, not relying on summaries by others. I began to feel that I understood a lot about international estate planning.

I had more and more clients with "foreign" assets who were referred to me by lawyers still back in the position I had been in a few years earlier.

One day I got a call from the niece of my original international estate planning client. "Uncle Henry just died. I'm named as his heir since he had no children. Can you help me sort out all of his assets?" I could!

I found a *notaire* in Paris who helped me with the tax and transfer of the Parisian apartment. I found a great lawyer in Rome who helped me with the villa outside Rome. I even went to the Isle of Jersey to find out how to transfer the flat in London that was owned by the company in Jersey.

I was stuck on a Swiss tax question though. The subject was the coordination of the U.S. estate tax and the Swiss inheritance tax. The U.S. approach is to tax the pool of assets owned by the person who died. In many European countries it works the other way around: the tax is charged against the various people who receive an inheritance.

Because there is no international rule in charge, each country is free to apply its own tax. For example, a person dying in the United States who leaves an inheritance to a daughter living in France could have double taxes: the U.S. tax would be against the assets and the French tax would be against the daughter. Because this seems "unfair" to many countries, there are a few estate tax treaties to avoid or at least lessen the double tax burden.

I now had a U.S. citizen client, who died while he had been living in Switzerland. This meant that each country would charge its tax. But I knew there is an estate tax treaty between Switzerland and the United States. I just couldn't figure out how to interpret the treaty, no matter how often I read it.

The purpose of tax treaties, in general, is to avoid having two countries tax the same person or the same assets. There are dozens of income tax treaties, and accounting firms are quite familiar with them. There are not very many treaties for estate or inheritance tax—it just doesn't get much attention. In the treatise I wrote I included the actual text of the sixteen treaties we do have. As others have remarked/complained, they are some of the most difficult legal documents to decipher. My cup of tea.

One of the key issues in the treaties is which country will actually collect the tax and which other country will have to allow a credit against its tax for the tax that was actually paid to the first country. I couldn't tell how it should work in the Swiss treaty. Several million dollars could go either way. The Swiss said they should be the ones to be paid first. Reading the language of the treaty, I wasn't so sure.

I said to the client the only way we could resolve this would be for me to go to Lausanne, Switzerland, to meet with the relevant tax office. Sure, she agreed, and so we both went. I took along a copy of the treaty, my French-English dictionary—just in case—and a copy of the preliminary tax forms. I also took a filled-out form based on winning our point of view.

The man who greeted me at the tax office acted surprised to see me. I guess I'd even say he acted fairly annoyed to see me. For my part, I felt that this time I just might be way out of my depth. They were, after all, the Swiss tax authorities. Switzerland has an enormous share of the world's private wealth—estimates are at one-third, though the information is hard to obtain.

They must know everything. Here I was, a lawyer from the state of Minnesota, wherever they might think that was, with no special authority. I also had no experience at all on these issues. It felt surreal just to be there.

The first man showed me into a small room and remained standing there while I sat down, gathered my papers, and stated my argument about how I thought one should read the treaty. I had to use my dictionary for part of that discussion. I showed him the language in the treaty that I thought should be read my way. I stayed seated at the table and waited for his reply.

Puzzled, he shrugged and left the room. He returned with two more men. I repeated my argument and showed them the relevant language in the treaty. They called for reinforcements—higher authorities, several more men. I stayed there at the table and repeated my argument. I was persistent: "I think this is how you should read the treaty."

I could hardly believe that I was sitting in the offices of the tax authorities of Switzerland, and I had the nerve to suggest that their reading of the treaty was not correct. They pointed to some secondary authorities. I pointed to the language of the treaty.

Guess what—they finally agreed with me! I was so excited, but not too excited to not remember to pull out the tax form I had already made out according to my version. I gave it to them to sign before I would leave. They signed the two copies and I took one with me—rejoicing in the victory! I felt like having a huge celebration.

The client was pleased but was much more interested in securing a good dinner reservation. I have never had the quality of food or burgundy wines as I did with her. I would work on the tax issues as we traveled, and she would work on the dinner reservations. We got the tax returns filed. Our view of the treaty was accepted. I was beginning to feel like an expert in international cstate planning. And we had a great dinner in Lausanne.

chapter three

"WE JUST LANDED IN BALI"

I STARED AT MY TEXT MESSAGE IN DISBELIEF! It was a quick reply to my text I had sent just two minutes earlier. Mine had said, "Just landed in Riyadh." In fact I had just landed at the airport in Riyadh, Saudi Arabia. I read it again. It still said, "Just landed in Bali."

The plane was still taxiing to the gate in Saudi Arabia, so I was already wearing my black *abaya*—the required covering black robe for all women in Saudi—in preparation for a week of meetings, starting with the man who apparently was now in Bali. Not in his office in Riyadh.

Meeting with him was the main reason for my trip. He had asked me: "Could you come to my office in Riyadh and review our various investment documents?"

At the time I was working in Zurich, so it wasn't as if I had flown all the way from my home in Minnesota to meet with

Abdul. But still. I had a very clear meeting date agreed to, for the very next day, in Riyadh. What did he mean, "Just landed in Bali"?

Well, it turned out to be true: he had just landed in Bali. I politely texted, "Didn't we have a meeting set in Riyadh for tomorrow?"

"I felt like taking our daughters and my wife to Bali for a few days in our jet. How long will you be in the Kingdom?"

I wasn't as shocked as I would have been before doing an increasing amount of international work. I had waited in a hotel lobby in Milan to be picked up for dinner "at 8 p.m." It was a long wait: he came at 9:30 p.m., acting perfectly normal. On the other hand in Tokyo I could hear a hotel staff member waiting just outside my door until the clock reached the time he was supposed to knock. Saudi taught me a new definition of "flexible."

Over the next several years, as I continued to do more and more work in Saudi with Saudi businessmen, I learned how challenging it was to make a fixed schedule with anyone. At the beginning I would email all of the contacts I wanted to meet with and would ask each one about their availability on a particular day and time. No one would commit. I finally developed a pattern of just letting all the possible people I might meet with know that I would be in the Kingdom during a certain range of dates.

"Would you like to set a meeting during the dates I will be there?" I tried this often: it never worked!

"I'm glad to know you are coming. I would love to meet. Yes. Just give me a call on my mobile when you are in the Kingdom." That was the standard reply. No help at all.

Years later I was commiserating with a seasoned Swiss banker who had worked with Saudis for decades; he knew exactly the problem of scheduling and shared his solution: "I always tell them I have already arrived in the Kingdom—when actually I might be only in Dubai."

I appreciated the advice, but never could bring myself to follow it.

The man who had just arrived in Bali became one of my longest term clients, and friends, in Saudi. He did come back from Bali while I was still in Riyadh and I did meet with him near the end of that trip of mine.

Over the years, he taught me a lot about Saudi culture, and also where they could use some of my help. It seemed common, for example, that investments with friends were done with little documentation, and it became hard to keep track of them all. Abdul gave me my own office in his building and my own computer, which was great. I did have to wear my *abaya* all day long, but not the head scarf. And there was a general bathroom I was welcome to use—which is sometimes an issue in Saudi as I had learned since there were few restrooms for women in some of the office buildings.

I settled in at my new office and started going through boxes of investment documents. I noted the places where I suggested there were some gaps that could be filled, such as signatures. Every day, I took my large black bag—black being the common and perhaps required color for women's accessories in Riyadh, which was known as the most orthodox region in all of Saudi.

In the bag I always carried some health snack bars since it would be quite brave of any Saudi men to have lunch with me in public, so I never knew whether there would be an invitation or not. There were just a few "safe" places where the feared religious police would not enter. Eating in a "mixed" setting—a man and a woman not married to each other—could in theory result in jail for both parties.

One of the safe places to eat, male and female, was the Four Seasons Hotel in Riyadh. Guards covered the doorways; cars and taxies were searched—including the trunks—at the entrance gates. I came to know the Four Seasons very well.

In my early trips to Riyadh it was my usual place to stay. They had a lunch buffet as expansive as any in the world. I loved being invited to lunch at the Four Seasons. Later I found alternate places to stay, especially the "ladies only" luxurious spa with limited overnight rooms. I clearly couldn't meet with any men there, so I continued to suggest that meetings—hopefully at lunch time—would be at the Four Seasons.

Even there one had to be careful though. The hotel was connected to a lovely high-end shopping mall, The Kingdom Center. In the connecting hallway from the hotel to the center was a new Starbucks. As everywhere the allure of Starbucks was that I would have a place to sit in peace and use their wi-fi.

It was the middle of the afternoon and I was in between appointments. So I chose a nice quiet table in the empty Starbucks and got out my iPhone.

"Lady, you may not sit there. Come over here to the other part, marked 'Family Section.'"

I knew by then that "family" meant single women too. The general entrance, unmarked, was assumed to be for men only. I sighed and resettled.

The Kingdom Center shopping mall carried all the famous clothing brands, and had a special fifth floor where no men were allowed. I saw some Saudi women take off their headscarves on that floor. Shopping was not a simple process though.

One day I needed a dressy skirt for a wedding I was invited to at the last minute. I arrived at the department store just as the long late-afternoon prayers began. The iron gates were pulled down at all the stores. I sat on a bench to wait until prayers were over. With very little time left, I quickly chose a skirt, but since all the salespeople were male I was not allowed to try it on anywhere. I had to buy it then take it outside to the restroom and try it on there. It did fit, and was at least "acceptable" at the lavish wedding.

I did make an exciting discovery one day in that same Kingdom Center whose shops I had nearly memorized by then. I spied a new Taco Bell there! One of my favorite fast food places. And, the largest eating section was a "families" room. I could go there, sit there, and enjoy my taste from home. My expat friends who lived in Riyadh did not know that a Taco Bell had opened—I shared my discovery with one of them.

While Beth and I were eating, I had some questions for her. We were sitting in an enclosed "family only" safe area. Why were all the women still wearing not only their *abayas,* which I had on also, but also their head scarves (I always found it difficult to eat while having it wrapped around my face) and in some cases they wore the black face coverings as well, which meant they had to lift up the black flap on their face each time they wanted to put a bite of food in their mouths. Beth had a ready explanation: someone might see them uncovered and report them back to their mother-in-law.

I spent a lot of time wandering around the Kingdom Center. I found a place to buy dates and pistachio nuts—to add to my in-room supply of snacks. I found a nice Samsonite luggage store, where I bought a new light suitcase to carry home two new carpets—which made it safely home in the airport plastic shrink wrapping I hadn't used before.

I was very glad to see that bag arrive in Minneapolis because when I checked it in in Riyadh the clerk had a long convoluted conversation with me about how I was going to too many places. The baggage tags had room for only two stops and I was making three stops. I thought I'd never see those carpets again. Now they are stunning on our city condo floor—another wonderful memory of so many great trips to Saudi Arabia.

As for the client who disappeared to Bali, I got used to it! So the next times I arrived for meetings, year after year—it didn't bother me at all to be told, "Sorry, our father has left the Kingdom for a while. How long will you be here?"

I could wait.

chapter four

"BUT WHAT DO YOU THINK, BARBARA?"

"SO, BARBARA, what was it like to clerk at the U. S. Supreme Court?"

I'm never sure how to answer this. It was exciting of course; it was also extremely confidential. After law school, a handful of graduates go on to clerk for federal judges. That clerkship is usually for one year. What the nature of the work is varies by the judge, but it usually involves reading the materials submitted for a case, writing short summaries of them, including a recommendation, and then writing the drafts of opinions.

"So what was it like at the U.S. Supreme Court?"

When I search for my own sense of what it was like, I remember vividly my first realization of the total power the Supreme Court has.

How are decisions made by a court? Our law schools are focused on court cases. Most of the time in law school is spent reading hundreds of cases and trying to draw broader conclusions from groups of cases. This "case method" is from England and is followed in that country and its former colonies, such as the United States. The rest of the world tends to have written "codes" of all the law—most of them based on the original Napoleonic Code from France.

I was a great student once I figured out how this case law method worked. I did very well in law school, busy searching for and studying cases. Even the classroom books are called "case" books. For exams I would memorize a number of the court holdings, ready to write them down in the exam booklet. I didn't really learn anything in law school about being a lawyer—but I did learn how to find cases.

What I was interested in were the appellate court opinions. These are the opinions that look at the legal rules—not the facts. I always found the facts a bit tedious, even boring, but I was fascinated by the arguments about what rule of law should apply. The best of our courts in the United States are the federal courts, so those are the best cases to study. I was living in the federal court territory covered by the Third Circuit Court of Appeals: Pennsylvania, Delaware, New Jersey and—yes this is true—the U.S. Virgin Islands.

When I graduated in 1976, most of my classmates went right into law firms. I was six years older than most students, having studied philosophy in graduate school and having two children by the time I went to law school. I wanted to keep studying appellate law. I remember a fellow law review student who was also a few years older saying he had no interest in applying for a clerkship after graduation. He challenged me, "Aren't you in a hurry to get started?" I wasn't. I loved studying the thinking behind the appellate opinions.

I was thrilled to be accepted for a one-year clerkship with a judge on the federal Court of Appeals for the Third Circuit. I had applied to several of them. One judge, whom I knew socially through his doctor son who worked with my husband, was appalled that I had applied for a clerkship with him. He knew I had two small children, a fact I never went out of my way to mention.

"Don't you know that children need their mothers full-time or they fail to develop?"

To cement his argument, he gestured with his hand high above the table: "There are many briefs to read."

Fortunately another judge seemed free of those prejudices. In fact when I went to his chambers for my interview with the other judge, his secretary said he was out on an errand—his daughter's typewriter needed repairs, so he had taken it out.

Each judge on the Third Circuit is located in a different city. My judge was based in what we always called "beautiful downtown Camden," New Jersey. My family lived out on the "main line" in the modest town of Narberth. I could take the train from Narberth, where the station was only two blocks from our house, to 30th Street station in Philadelphia, change to the New Jersey train and get off in the heart of (dangerous) Camden.

The judge kept very standard hours; I was never late getting home. In the winter when it was dark early, though, he did have an annoying insistence on walking me to the train station, which he didn't do for the male clerk. And he did enjoy a chuckle on court days when he made sure to show me that the tie under his long black robe had a cute little pink "male chauvinist pig" all across it.

And there was the day at lunch when he was telling a story about another judge who had put in his opinion a footnote chastising one of the lawyers for referring to the other lawyer as "Toots." The judge saw the instant distaste on my face and laughed. He loved giving nicknames to all his clerks—and now I had mine!

Cleaning out boxes of papers from those days, I recently found and kept all the memos and later letters, even when I was at law firms, addressed to "Toots." Otherwise he was really great, and I learned a lot.

By definition the only cases that came to the Third Circuit already had the facts agreed upon, the disputes were only about the right law to apply. I used my law school case search skills every single day. The difference was that we really didn't care too much what most other judges had decided, unless the opinions were by the Supreme Court, of course. At that time there were eleven circuits across the United States. I always began my research with a search of "similar" cases in the other circuits.

Our job as clerks was to read the lower court opinions and all of the supporting briefs that might be filed. The very first part we looked at was the date the appeal was filed. If it happened to be filed late—we could to toss it, no need to read. Then we did our own research, searching all those cases again. Finally we wrote a short, one-page summary memo regarding what the issue of law was and how we thought it should be resolved. After the full court met, heard arguments and voted, one judge was assigned to write the opinion. His clerk would write the first draft. They would circulate it to the other judges for comments and changes, and a final opinion would be written. Our judge included his clerks in the voting process if there was an opinion we did not want to write, we would ask him to "shoestring it." During the voting he would fiddle with tying his shoes, with his head down.

Part of what I learned from the judge was to keep it simple and clear when writing. He loved to edit memos by breaking up long paragraphs into very short sections. I still think of him when I try to do the same.

Another was his consistent lack of assuming, as he well could, that he was quite important. I remember several times while meeting with him in his "chambers" when the phone rang. The chambers were a string of separate office areas, all lined with impressive bookshelves. He had the largest room, of course. His secretary sat in the next office area. After her, each of us clerks had the next adjacent offices. The rest was our library.

When the phone rang, the judge just liked to answer it himself. That was not protocol and did not please his secretary who would lunge to try to get the phone first. I could just imagine the faces of the lawyers on the other end who were not prepared for the chummy phone answer of "Jim here."

Once I even heard this: "Jim here. No, that's not the right number. Who are you trying to call? Let me get out my phone book and look it up for you."

On special days he would bring in split pea soup he had made at home. It was a wonderful year.

Next, yes I did apply for another appellate clerkship, this one at the very top of the legal profession: the United States Supreme Court. Hooray I was accepted. Alas that judge retired before I began. Hooray another judge added me to his own clerks.

At this court they are no longer called judges. They are all called justices. Most would have four clerks, nearly all of whom would have spent the prior year clerking for a federal appellate judge, as I had. As the year went on, I became visibly the first pregnant clerk in the history of the court! Whenever that was mentioned, I would add in my head that this was with child number three. No one mentioned my increasingly obvious status.

My first week at the Supreme Court I was ready to practice

the case search skills I had developed so well. I was assigned one of the cases to bring to our group discussion in the justice's chambers. It was actually a totally boring case, about interpreting part of the regulations that apply to longshoremen, the people who load and unload at the docks. Nonetheless I had done the job I knew how to do. I had found the similar cases by other circuits. When it was my turn for discussion, I started with, "The Fourth Circuit held 'yes' and the Fifth Circuit held 'no.'"

The justice stopped me, holding up his hand. "But what do you think we should do, Barbara?"

This took my breath away. The realization hit me: this is "the" court in the country. They are free to make the decision they think is the right one. I would have to think differently going forward. No longer was it a search for the relevant cases. Now it was time to think about the law, and what it should be, and why.

The Supreme Court in 1976.

"What was it like to clerk at the Supreme Court?"

"It was amazing, and it was humbling."

chapter five

"TELL THE WIDOW TO WEAR RED"

I WAS UP ON THE STAGE IN LONDON, at the very grand and very large Langham Hotel, along Hyde Park, in one of their ornate ballrooms. As the leader of our panel at the annual Congress of the prestigious international lawyers' group, the Union Internationale des Avocats (UIA).

I looked out at the well-dressed lawyers from all over the world. Our panel's topic was about international estate planning, specifically about the legal rules that applied when someone dies. Several years earlier I had founded the Commission on International Estate Planning in the UIA, so I was Madam President; it was a very formal group. Each year the annual Congress was held in a different location.

Our commission's first meeting had been in Marrakesh. This year it was in London. We were always a serious, technical, detailed group of lawyers.

I was taking questions from the audience of more than 200 lawyers from around the world. One of the issues that had been raised by our panel was how different countries handled bank accounts and safe deposit boxes upon the death of the owner.

For example, in the United States, there are no uniform federal rules: it is a matter for each state to decide. Almost all states would have an executor appointed and the court would supervise the collection of the assets. A safe deposit box would be sealed on the death of the owner, and only the executor would have access, perhaps after posting a bond. Sometimes there would be a requirement that someone from the tax authority must also be present. The tax risk, of course, would be that someone otherwise entitled to open the box would do so and take the assets out and not declare them. This would often apply to jewelry since possession easily looked like ownership. Other countries have different rules.

What has always intrigued me about international estate planning is the lack of coordination when more than one country is involved. For example, for many years it was possible to arrange a Japanese wealthy person's plan so that a Japanese child would come to live in the United States, maybe for college or later, while the wealthy parent stayed in Japan, owning substantial assets in Japan. Then the parent would make a large gift to the child, usually several million U.S. dollars.

The way the gift tax system worked in Japan was that it would tax only the person who received the gift. On the other hand the gift tax system in the United States was just the opposite and would only tax the person who made the gift. So the wealthy parent could have passed on the wealth to the child with no Japanese gift tax and no U.S. gift tax. The plan seemed almost too good to be true. It took Japan a while to figure out how to prevent this, which it eventually did, and changed its laws.

Another quirk with Japan was that when someone died in Japan, there would be a tax on all that they owned. This did not apply to short-term visitors, but it did seem to apply to anyone who had lived in Japan more than one year. Many of the non-Japanese expats living in Japan worried about this. I remember at another conference I had asked a Japanese tax lawyer what advice he would have for an American living in Japan more than a year, but was still there on a temporary basis, if her husband died while in Japan.

With all of the knowledge of the Japanese tax systems he had, here is the advice he gave: "Tell her to leave Japan, fast. Tell her to go home."

Part of the fun of international estate planning, for me, is paying attention to the cultural attitudes, which can vary a lot. One of my first encounters with a different cultural attitude was when I was in Rome to obtain a local appraiser's valuation of a villa that had been owned by an American client who had died.

The client had filed a local registry statement that he was a legal resident of Rome. However he was also a U.S. citizen. The United States is quite aggressive in imposing its estate (death) tax on its citizens, wherever they might live. Citizens are subject to a U.S. estate tax on all of their worldwide assets.

Almost all other countries in the world apply that worldwide tax on assets only if the person was a legal resident of that country. Here in my Italian case we had the worst of both worlds. The United States would apply its tax on all assets. Italy would apply its tax on all assets. A treaty might help to limit the damage, but the cases were serious.

In any event the United States would insist on a proper

valuation of all of the assets and collect its tax. A major asset was the villa just outside Rome. I was working with the Rome lawyer who had been recommended by the U.S. embassy, someone who turned out to be quite experienced, and someone I enjoyed working with on other matters for many years afterward. I got to know his family and was a guest in their apartment and in their country home on the seaside. I thought we were similar people and similar lawyers—until we got to the tax issues.

He told me, "I'll include only the Italian assets on my Italian tax return. I won't mention all the others."

"But," I said, "under Italian law when the deceased person was a resident of Italy, aren't you supposed to include all the worldwide assets?"

"Well, yes," he said, "but that is too much trouble and will just confuse the authorities, and then under the treaty we would end up with only the Italian assets anyway, so I am just making it simpler for everyone."

This was, I must admit, a different approach to me. But he was the Italian lawyer and I was not.

We did agree that we had to have a value for the Italian villa. I was never sure he understood what I kept saying—that it had to be a "fair market" value. The United States tax authorities had offices in several major European cities favored by Americans, including Rome, and they were known to be suspicious of low valuations on foreign assets, especially homes.

I wanted to avoid an audit by the U.S. Internal Revenue Service. My strategy was to offer a local Italian market appraisal on the U.S. tax return, which might lead them to decide that to challenge it would not be worthwhile.

I finally came to Rome in person to meet with the lawyer and a local appraiser he had arranged to meet with us. At our meeting,

I kept trying to explain to both of them what "fair market" value means.

I had memorized the definition back in law school—fair market value is "the price that a willing buyer would pay a willing seller, neither under duress nor obligation."

The appraiser didn't seem to follow me. He kept pointing to a published schedule of values. Those values just seemed too low to me.

So I kept asking in different ways: "How much would someone pay to buy it?"

He pointed to the schedule again. I said, "Is that all they would pay?"

Suddenly the light went on and he said, "Oh you mean what this scheduled amount is and also the extra amount that is paid under the table?"

Yes indeed. That was what I wanted. So we filed with a very fair looking Italian appraisal market value attached, and there was no IRS audit.

I was thinking of this Italian example during our London UIA conference, and the question of how different countries treat bank accounts on the death of the owner.

I had been surprised to learn, for example, that with Swiss bank accounts, even when they were registered to a married couple as joint owners, on the death of one spouse the bank would freeze the account. The surviving spouse would have to file papers to have access to the joint account, which could be a very lengthy process.

In most states in the United States the other joint owner is required to report the death and the bank will then seal the safe deposit box, to be opened only in the presence of a tax representative, as mentioned above. I was standing in the middle of the stage, chairing the panel, as we talked about different legal approaches to this issue. We were all, as usual, quite serious and very focused on describing the technical law in various countries.

Then, in the back of the room, a lawyer stood up, said she was from Spain, and announced with certainty she had come up with a very practical plan, which she was happy to share with us. Her solution was to advise the widow to go to the bank quickly and to empty the joint accounts without mentioning that her husband had died. To clinch her advice she told us all:

"I tell the widow to wear red!"

chapter six

"ARISTOTLE AND SKIN WALKERS"

SOMETHING WAS WRONG. I couldn't figure out what. It was my first night teaching in Gallup, New Mexico, in the four-room branch of the University of New Mexico. I came with a great education: philosophy major at Wellesley College, master's degree in philosophy at the Chicago Circle Campus of the University of Illinois, teaching assistant, Ph.D. underway, etc. So what was wrong?

We had arrived on the Navajo Reservation at the small government-built outpost in Northwest New Mexico, 135 miles from Albuquerque. My husband Doug would be working as a Public Health Service doctor for two years, as an alternative to Vietnam. I knew I would be having some free time, so we also planned for the birth of our first child to occur a few months after our arrival on the reservation.

By the end of the first year I really wanted an academic life again. I had been working on my Ph.D., but the long distance from the university made it all seem quite unreal.

Everything was different from Chicago, our first married home for two years, and from our recent year in the Bronx. I had attended philosophy classes at Columbia, Doug had his internship in a big city hospital, and I could visit my "upper east side" grandparents—it was fun to live in New York, the city where I had been born.

The Vietnam draft was a scary part of the planning landscape then. Doug had hoped to join the Navy, but they rejected him as soon as they learned that he had a wife studying philosophy at Columbia. Unacceptably radical. A friend suggested the Public Health Service and its Indian reservations. My parents lived in New Mexico so the Navajo reservation in New Mexico seemed a good fit, even though they were at the opposite corner of the large state, a seven-hour drive or one hour in their small plane.

One of the neighbors came over and watched me unpack boxes the movers had left. I was glad to see the box that had our impressive double deadlock bolt from our Bronx apartment.

"What in the world is that?" she asked.

She explained that no one locked their doors. She made me feel too embarrassed to ever install it, though I worried the whole first year that it wasn't installed, and I always did lock the simple lock that was built in to our front door, even though everyone seemed to have keys to all the homes.

Another item we decided not to connect was our television set. We stored it in a bedroom closet unplugged for the two years we were on the reservation. It seemed only fair to be 100% on the reservation and not look at regular television news. The Navajo nation was, at some 200,000 people, the largest Indian reservation in the United States. We would live as quiet visitors in their nation.

Our new town consisted of four square blocks of government stucco housing in high mesa country. You could look out past the paved four blocks and see where the paved road ended abruptly into dirt, with mesas on all sides. Four doctors and their wives, all from big-city training came for the two years, the older ones teaching the newer ones. There was one dentist and his wife and one pharmacist and his wife, as well as one all-round handyman and his wife. Our small group was labeled "the Anglos." The Navajos were simply "the people."

Our Public Health Service hospital was for Navajos. It lacked some basics like blood and oxygen. We had planned to have the baby delivered at the big hospital, in Gallup, also a Navajo hospital.

When I went for my checkup there, the first question was, "What part of blood are you?" I had to think about that: my correct answer was "none."

When our baby was born, the staff felt so sorry for him because he didn't have a thick head of black hair; they kept wrapping a towel around his head.

This was also during the era of "back to Mother Earth" and compost gardening. I still have the original Whole Earth catalogue I ordered from. Essentials like a cherrywood spinning wheel from New Zealand, bags of raw wool to card and spin—not that I knew how to do any of that. More essentials like a set of glass-cutting tools to take the top off of glass Coke bottles and turn them into usable glasses. A step above that was to glue the tops onto the bottom half of the bottle and make wine glasses with stems. I also sewed, including toddler clothes for our son, who wasn't particular about how his clothes looked.

My husband was on call almost all the time it seemed. He'd come home, just one block from the small government hospital, and fall into bed. He'd get up, eat, and go back to the hospital. In spite of that schedule, he was able to spend time befriending some of the Navajos as he made his rounds on the pitted rutted dirt roads out to small settlements, taking medicine and water and the advice to breastfeed. Apparently missionary groups had pushed formula milk, but the unclean water meant a very high infant mortality rate.

Doug was especially pleased to make friends with the local medicine man, Manuelito Begay, whose picture hangs in Doug's office today. He and the medicine man developed a respectful professional relationship: patients whose diseases were not clear were referred to the medicine man. In turn he referred those who wanted x-rays—a very popular treatment—or who were clearly terminal to be sent to the Western doctor. If someone died in a hogan, the eight-sided dwelling of adobe and wood, it would have to be destroyed. Much more efficient to die in the hospital. When the clinic added some space, Manuelito gave it a blessing ceremony.

For my part, there was a limit to my interest, not to mention my low skill level, in the satisfaction I could get from spinning and sewing. I was getting tired of gathering compost elements from the neighbors' garbage. I missed academics. I missed studying.

I had been teaching in Chicago as a graduate student and was looking forward to doing it again.

I finally found the right person to contact. Could I teach a class in Gallup? What was my subject again, he asked. I am pretty sure he was not at all clear about what "philosophy" was. He kept calling it "psychology." He himself taught golf. He also didn't know why I would want to drive the sixty miles to Gallup to teach when I had a husband who was a doctor. "Oh," he finally said, "you want some 'pin money.'" I bristled at his use of the pejorative term, used for a housewife's extra spending money, not for earned money from teaching, for example. But I didn't say anything; I wanted the job.

In the end he agreed that I could teach an evening class on philosophy. He said he'd stop by sometime to see how it went, but he never did.

I was excited to have a full class signed up. About half the class was adult Navajos, all men, several of them from the tribal police force earning extra college credits. The other half were young men from the Catholic seminary near Albuquerque, 135 miles to the east. It didn't matter to me who the students were. I would be teaching the same material I had taught before as a graduate student in Chicago.

I knew how to teach this subject, so I said "hello" to the class and went right ahead.

At the time I believed—as in I knew—that my education had been one of the finest in the country, so I had no qualms about facing a new, and somewhat different, group of students.

I still remember that first class. I began with Plato, and moved right on to Aristotle—seeing that in print now makes me think I was really absurd to barge ahead with those particular subjects.

I was talking and talking to that first class. I was busy sharing my knowledge about the role of Plato and the role of Aristotle. I was sure I was doing an excellent job. But I did notice that the students did not look happy. They were looking at each other. They looked more and more puzzled—and I had no idea why.

Finally one student raised his hand. I was so relieved. Now I would be able to find out what was wrong.

"These people you are talking about, didn't they have any real jobs?" That was the question.

Wow. I wasn't sure what to say. I think I meandered around, talking about the importance of asking those "important" questions in philosophy. I doubt if I persuaded anyone that night.

I went home, thinking on my long drive that I should have been able to answer that. I should not have assumed during all my education that the validity and importance of traditional Western philosophy was obvious. I should be able to back up several levels and be able to start with a justification of the relevance of philosophy in general.

What a wonderful, if startling, discovery that was. From then on I have always tried to begin with the basic context, and go from there, no matter what the subject is. A saying I heard years later would have been useful to apply then: "Never underestimate your audience's intelligence; never overestimate their knowledge."

The next class I had to begin again, in a much more humble attitude. We could think about what philosophical questions were about. What did it mean to know something? How could we know that we know? I assigned papers to be written on those subjects.

When the papers were turned in, I didn't know what to think. The students had clearly been listening to me, but their papers were filled with the sightings of "skin walkers" and their significance. Of course I had never heard of skin walkers. Apparently they were from the next world, as the spirits of those who had died. I had no idea how to fit that in with the teachings of Aristotle. I was clearly in over my head.

I didn't want to give up, though, and neither did the students. When it was time for a new semester I went further out and offered two courses: one in western logic and one on Hume's

Dialogues Concerning Natural Religion. Hume was quite skeptical about our knowledge of the existence of god.

Teaching the Venn circle diagrams of logic seemed to go okay. Hume's skepticism did not. Suddenly the seminary students were on high alert. Hume's skepticism had them running to their bishop in Albuquerque in between our classes. They would come up to my desk before a class and tell me that Hume, and I, had been wrong—because the bishop said it was different. I would answer that claim, and before the next class I'd be informed of another answer from the bishop. It was fun to have those dialogues with the students, and the bishop in absentia.

Meanwhile the Navajo students let my Western teachings go right out the window. At the next paper-writing time the subjects were logic and Hume. The papers I received were filled with stories of "skin walkers." I clearly had more to learn.

A Navajo Hogan

chapter seven

WHY I HAVE MY VERY OWN BEFANA

SHE HANGS BEHIND MY SHOULDER, on the top edge of the French door to my home study, watching me always. She is made of felt, about three feet long, with a red long skirt with a white apron over it and she grips a broomstick made of real twigs. My very own Befana. I brought her back—she packed flat—from a work trip to Rome for a law firm client one early December.

I remember that trip with a smile. I should have known by then I would not have a lot of success scheduling meetings in Rome in early December. As with other holidays in Italy, back then people took a generous amount of time off. Time to get ready for the holidays, the holidays themselves, and then time to recover from the holidays. Bureaucrats in particular, who had limited work hours in the busiest of times, seemed to vanish. And I had to meet with some tax authority bureaucrats, so I was advised to slow down. I had been there a few times by then.

At the beginning of that particular week in Italy I was "all business." I had come to sort out some of the legal questions for a client's properties in Italy. By the middle of that week, though, I gave up and was just enjoying the decorations, the atmosphere, and the festive mood all around. The legal questions could wait.

Walking absentmindedly into the entrance to the Piazza Navona, one of my favorite squares in Rome, I stopped and stared. It had been transformed and I didn't recognize anything.

Nothing remained of the classic view of the fountains, with the Roman racecourse oval around them both. Instead every meter was covered by wooden and canvas booths—they were all selling nativity scenes and other Christmas decorations.

I walked up and down the paths between them. I had never seen so many nativity scenes. I wanted to buy a lot of them! I had only my carry-on luggage, so I finally chose a small nativity scene, complete with a roof over the manger, which I still enjoy taking out each Christmas at home.

The nativity scene sits on our glass table at Christmas right next to a jolly cardboard-based large Father Christmas that I managed to squash without much harm and pack home from a work trip to the Isle of Man.

When I look at him, I smile thinking of the taxi driver I had on my first trip to the Isle of Man, a speck in the North Irish Sea but an important international tax jurisdiction—sometimes called a tax haven, which was not unrelated to my reason for being there. He joked when he picked me up that I must have my suitcase full of money—"Everyone comes here for money transactions," he said as he chuckled.

He had a worldly air I thought, living in one of the prime offshore international financial centers. He probably did drive people from around the world with suitcases filled with cash. That sophisticated image I had of him went out the window when he slowed down over a small bridge in the countryside and blew kisses from his fingertips, explaining that "you must greet the fairies who live under the bridge."

I should add that I have never believed in fairies, or spirits, or angels—or anything unseen and not consistent with my rigorous view of logic. I had even taught logic a few times.

But I look at my Befana, watching my back, and I smile at the jolly Father Christmas on our glass table—and then realize how many, dozens and dozens, of small creatures I have brought back from so many trips and so many places.

Father Christmas sits right next to a gorgeous white and gold papier-mâché angel I brought back from a trip to visit our son in his Canadian boarding school. Sometimes I keep her on the table long past Christmas, long into our Minnesota winter. I just realized that she reminds me of the Ice Queen in the children's story.

I began the collection of small figures with some *kachina* dolls when we lived on the Navajo reservation and added a storyteller doll from the nearby Pueblo reservation. The local Navajos made soft dolls of adult men and women with their native velvet tops and dresses complete with an assortment of silver belts and necklaces. I collected several of each.

When I started going to Japan on a frequent basis, my doll collection took on a new life. How to choose from so many very lovely dolls. Each village had their own styles. I don't think there was any trip to Japan that did not include my carrying back at least one new doll. I especially liked the wooden ones: round and squat or thin and tall, I loved them all. I found a neighborhood in Tokyo that was dedicated to dolls of all kinds. I bought some there too.

Today a plaster painted two-foot high kneeling Japanese woman protects my husband and me from her position on our bed's headboard at our country home. In the city apartment we are watched over by five wildly colorful dragon heads I brought back from a trip to Hong Kong.

I keep collecting these small figures wherever I go. On my work desk there's a small "whirling dervish" from a conference in Istanbul. There's a Chinese fisherman from Guilin on his bamboo boat with his cormorant bird nearby. A carved family of the tall Maasai and their children are a reminder of the safari trip we enjoyed in Tanzania. There's a joyous blue Venetian glass figure near a window from a solo winter trip I made to the Piazza San Marco.

From a conference in Prague I added to my Russian nesting dolls, of which I might have too many now. Each one has a different design. From Hurgada, Egypt I brought back seven small clay everyday work figures. From Mumbai, where I spoke at a conference, I had time to buy a beautifully decorated ceramic elephant head to hang on the wall in honor of Ganesh the elephant god.

In Saudi Arabia at an expat fair I found a glass ball for a Christmas tree—a forbidden holiday in Saudi—with a lovely camel painted on it. It now hangs on the doorknob just below my Befana. On a shelf in the living room is a bejeweled and loaded camel, a gift from a Saudi man. Newest are two trolls from a trip to Norway: one is tall and wooden; the other is shorter and made of wool with only a red nose showing. There are more, but you probably get the idea.

Back to Befana. The one I have, brought back from that Piazza Navona Christmas display, is a cheerful creature made of cloth to be hung. The legend about her is said to go back thousands of years. When the three magi were on their way to visit the baby Jesus, Befana chose to stay behind but realized later she should have gone, so she flew on her broom with a bag of gifts, which she would go down the chimneys to deliver. For the good children there was candy; for the bad children there was coal.

As happens so often the children's holiday explanation has other layers beneath it. In the case of Befana, I learned that her name is the Greek word for "epiphany" which is a religious holiday celebrated on January 6th.

Since the 1300s there have been purifying rites that day; it is said that water prepared that evening, the evening that Befana begins her trip, can ward off evil spirits. For my part, I decided a while ago not to put my Befana away after Christmas. She hangs on my study door all year long.

Why did I want to write now about Befana and the others? As a child I didn't play much with dolls. These figures I've been collecting seem different. Why did I even want to have "my own" Befana?

To me, they are like spirits from so many of my travels. Each is a reminder of another time and another place. They seem to have their own characters.

Am I starting to understand that taxi driver who greeted the fairies who live under the bridge?

chapter eight

BORN A EUNUCH?

"DON'T WORRY ABOUT THE DANCERS," said our guide in India. I looked again. The seven dancers were whirling around in colorful swirls of silk saris, under the dark night sky, lit by a dozen torch lights behind the dancers. Why should I worry or not worry about the dancers?

Our group of international lawyers, with some spouses, was in the northwest Rajasthan region of India, on a post-conference trip following our annual meeting in New Delhi, where I had just finished chairing the commission on international estate planning. My husband joined us for the post-conference week-long trip on the Palace on Wheels, a maharaja restored train, similar to the Orient Express.

The evening dancers, eye-catching in the empty desert, all looked like beautiful, graceful women—but the guide had just informed us, "By the way, they are all eunuchs."

I'm guessing that most in our group were as shocked as I was and that it showed. "Don't worry about them," our guide added. "They are born eunuchs."

Liberal as I considered myself to be, this was too much for me. The guide's statement had crossed a line. Someone cannot physically be born a eunuch! I thought eunuchs came into being only by the males being castrated—involuntarily.

So I did some research. I focused on India, where I learned that eunuchs are called *hijras* and that there may be as many as two million of them in India. And, indeed, I was right that the most common way of "becoming" a eunuch was involuntary castration.

The ancient value of eunuchs was that they could be trusted to guard harems, presenting no sexual male threat.

It gets more complicated though. In India there seem to be extensive communities of *hijras*, when a young male, otherwise a fully equipped male, can become assimilated and cared for by that community, when he has no one else to care for him.

The *hijras* have created a role for themselves. They often attend births and ask for contributions. Ironically the *hijras* today in India are sometimes seen as good candidates to run for public office: they will not be influenced by loyalty to their children. They have no children, of course.

In 2014 the Supreme Court of India actually ruled that for all official registrations an additional category would be added: in addition to "male" or "female," one could also register as "third sex." One politician made an innovative argument that eunuchs, as an extension of their historical role guarding harems, should be used to protect the borders of India.

Puzzling over the "born a eunuch" claim led me to a new attempt to be able to list basic human rights, regardless of country or culture. In fact, the reason I had joined the legal group that had arranged the now unforgettable dance in the desert by eunuchs was because of its dedication to the global defense of human rights. It was in San Francisco that I attended my first meeting, the first time they had a meeting in the United States after I had joined a few years earlier. I was curious about the committee called "The Status of the Woman." Now I understand that the very title was quite French—it sounded odd in English.

I was expecting more of the usual "women's rights" issues I had encountered my whole adult life. Why were there so few women as partners in law firms? Why were there so few women on the boards of major companies? And so on.

I went in the room and took a seat. I noticed right away that the majority of the people in the room were men. That was different. Then I heard the issue they were debating: "What could be done to stop the practice of female genital mutilation?"

Female what? I had never heard the term. They were familiar with it, referring to "FGM" and describing various court victories they had in France. These were not the lawyers I was used to in U.S. legal groups, where more of the focus was on how to gain more clients and increase the law firm's revenue.

To educate myself about human rights I found and read through the United Nations' Universal Declaration of Human Rights. What an amazing document. Article 16 was especially interesting to me:

> The family is the natural and fundamental group unit of society and is entitled to protection by society and the State.

And relating to governance, a specialty of mine, this is in Article 21:

> (3) The will of the people shall be the basis of the authority of government; this will shall be expressed in periodic and genuine elections which shall be by universal and equal suffrage and shall be held by secret vote or by equivalent free voting procedures.

This led me to the United Nations Convention on the Rights of the Child. This awesome document has been adopted, according to the official website, by every country in the world—except Somalia and the United States.

I was surprised to read that children have a right to be named—something I had never thought about.

The full text of that article 7 is:

> The child has the right to a name at birth. The child also has the right to acquire a nationality and, as far as possible, to know his or her parents and be cared for by them.

I love seeing in print that children have a "right" to be cared for by their parents. I wish the United States had adopted it.

I became a strong supporter of the legal group I had discovered in that San Francisco meeting. Right away I encountered an unusual twist. The head of the U.S. group asked, "Barbara, can you be a speaker at the next annual conference, scheduled to take place in Marrakech, Morocco?"

"Sure, I'd love to." I had never been to Morocco and would enjoy going there.

"Which committee would you speak in?"

I had to answer, "I don't seem to fit in any committee. My field is estate planning, and you don't seem to have estate planning."

I had read the list of committees several times. I didn't fit anywhere. The committees ranged from human rights—including the intriguingly named "The Defense of the Defense"—to multinational corporate transactions.

"I could speak, but we would need a new committee on my subject."

The committees were actually called "commissions," and I was informed rather strongly that one doesn't just waltz in and create a commission. "It would take several years to have a new commission approved."

First it would present itself as a "working group"; then, if after a few years, it was looking solid enough, it could apply for the status of becoming a "commission." Okay, understood.

My best option was to form a new working group in Marrakech, on "International Laws of Succession." I invited a lawyer I knew from Switzerland, one from Italy, one from Austria, and a *notaire* from Paris. I should explain that in Europe the legal profession is roughly divided into two categories. One is the *avocats* (the lawyers), who handle a variety of regular legal issues; the second is the *notaires*, who handle most of the estate and inheritance issues. The word *notaire* translates as notary, which gets very confusing to U.S. lawyers, who are familiar with notaries whose role is to swear to someone's identity, period. In France, and other civil law countries, the *notaires* have a training similar to that of lawyers.

The legal organization I was working with was, and is, called the Union Internationale des Avocats. Aha, the title did not include *notaires* and that is why my estate planning issues didn't belong anywhere.

I made the mistake that first year in Marrakech of asking the authorities if I could include a *notaire* on my panel. I was told no. But my invited *notaire* wasn't disheartened; he went ahead and sent in his membership fee, which was duly accepted. For the first time in the history of the organization we presented a mixed panel—lawyers and a *notaire*.

Our working group in Marrakech was a hit! We had great attendance and great interest. The organization was impressed. They decided at their next governing board meeting that we could go ahead and advance early—we could be an official commission! And guess who was named the Madam President of the new commission. It's a role I have thoroughly enjoyed, right up to the time I finally had been elected the maximum number of years. Now I am permanently the Madam President Emeritus. I like the title.

Back to my curiosity about eunuchs. Now that I was in a group that put a high value on justice and human rights, I started thinking about whether there were any human rights issues in the inheritance field. I thought of a few. I might include some of the built-in preferences given to male children, like the old English inheritance rules of primogeniture, which gave the entire inheritance to the oldest son. Or the need to have a son inheritor that still is strong enough in Japan to justify adopting an adult son if one is lacking. I might be able to include the "inheritance" of titles or even being born into certain cultures. Maybe I could turn this topic into a law review article?

I had been wanting to write a law review article on some topic and shift my time more into teaching in law school. To have published law review articles was a key to being accepted on most faculties. The articles tended to be long, detailed, and filled with more footnotes than text in some cases. Rather intimidating, and very hard to get published in one.

Now, sparked by that evening in Rajasthan with the lovely dancers under the stars, I had my fetching title: "Born a Eunuch? Harmful Inheritance Practices and Human Rights." I had fun doing some creative research. And it was accepted for publication in *Law & Inequality: A Journal of Theory and Practice.* Hooray!

I owed it all to the guide who had explained so matter-of-factly: "Don't worry about them. They are born eunuchs."

chapter nine

I TAUGHT FAR EASTERN RELIGIONS TO . . . THE MAFIA?

HOW IN THE WORLD DID I GET IN THIS SITUATION? I was standing in front of a skeptical classroom of adult students in night classes at Glassboro State College in New Jersey.

When my husband and I were still living on the Navajo reservation and I was still hanging on to my Ph.D. studies in philosophy while caring for our first child, I started planning for our move to Philadelphia. My husband was set with his medical residency in Philadelphia that would last several years. But what would I do?

Having a master's degree in Philosophy, which I had, was not a guaranteed entry into the teaching world—as I quickly learned.

In fact it didn't seem to be an asset anywhere. That became obvious as I received rejection after rejection to my offers to teach philosophy anywhere in or near Philadelphia. Finally I got one "nibble"—Glassboro State College (must be somewhere in New Jersey, I thought) was looking for a full-time experienced professor in "Far Eastern religions" to be a tenured professor, which is someone with solid experience who had published law review articles on Far Eastern religions.

I knew absolutely nothing about any Far Eastern religion. I couldn't even name them if I had to. So I applied for the job.

They must not have had many other applicants. They replied, tactfully, that although I did not seem qualified enough to fill the tenure position, they could interview me about teaching an evening class on Far Eastern religions. My best offer. My only offer.

We moved to Philadelphia and I went to the interview at Glassboro State College, which seemed to be in Glassboro New Jersey, a bit of a drive from Philadelphia. By then I was pregnant, though not visibly, with our second child. I certainly didn't mention that in my interview. I was accepted.

First stop—a bookstore to find some books about Far Eastern religions. At college we had a required freshman course in biblical studies, but that was my grand total of my knowledge of religions of any sort. I had been raised as a Presbyterian, but there was nothing there to help me with Far Eastern religions.

I found a book, a perfect book. It had summaries of all possible Far Eastern religions. Whew. I had a plan. For each week's class I could first read the chapter on that religion, then "explain" it to the students.

The students were not an easy group. They were all adults, and they were always skeptical of whatever I was saying. They had a camaraderie with each other, but none with me. Once again I felt

I was in front of a very foreign culture.

I got some inkling of how much I was out of my depth when I asked everyone to say their names at the first class. About halfway through a student said his name was Joe G-xxx. The whole class gasped and laughed nervously. When I got home that night I asked my husband what that was about. I guess everyone except me knew that was a major Mafia name. Swell.

I carried on, religion after religion. Buddhism, Taoism, Confucianism, Shinto, Jainism, and so on. I think the class tolerated me, at best.

The man who had interviewed me had warned me that he planned to sit in on one of my classes. I kept wondering if that would happen. Several months into the course I was by then quite visibly pregnant.

In fact that was the only topic that seemed to interest my students. During break they would come up and ask when the baby was due. During class they started asking what my own religion was. I would never answer that question. It turns out that they were all very Catholic. They started telling me they were worried that if I didn't have the baby properly christened it would go to hell. Great.

About then the man who had interviewed me walked into the class I was teaching. I worked hard to do a better-than-average job. I thought the class went pretty well. Then the break came and he hurried up to the front to talk to me. I was waiting for a compliment. Not so. He could hardly control himself and blurted out the accusation: "You are pregnant."

Well, that was obviously true. He made it clear that there was no way they would ask me to continue for the following term. End of my Far Eastern religions teaching career.

I still have the book I used, but I still don't remember anything about the various religions. I gave up on a career of teaching philosophy and applied to law schools.

I look back and wonder what I learned from that experience. Did I learn not to teach something I didn't know? I guess not. In law school I sort of did it again.

There was a liberal-sounding city program where law students in Philadelphia could volunteer to teach in local high schools. One of the schools on the list was the University High School. With the word "University" in its name, it sounded classy and easy to me, so that was the school I signed up for. It was also a short walk from the law school.

As background, I should have thought about the fact that the law school was known to be in a very dangerous part of the city. I had to walk four blocks to get the train home each day, and in the winter, walking in the dark, I remember worrying that I could be attacked and they might steal my briefcase with my study notes.

The starting date I had signed up for came. I found the high school. I walked up to the front door. It was locked with chains threaded through the handles. I walked around to find an open door. None. I went back to the front door and pulled at it, rattling the chains.

Finally a woman came to the other side of the door and opened it a crack. What did I want? I introduced myself. "Fine," she said. "Wait while I get a student to escort you." Some faint alarm bells went off—why did I need an escort?

My escort came and walked me to a classroom. This time I had prepared for the subject I would be teaching. As in the Glassboro teaching experience, I had not studied the subject before, but this subject sounded a lot easier to handle than F Eastern religions. It was supposed to be a class on how our government works—as in, we have three branches of government, which I sketched on the chalkboard. Oh, oh. I suddenly realized that to write on the chalkboard I had to turn my back to the students.

I had been told I would be teaching the elite class, the college-bound students. I saw they didn't like to sit in their chairs. They were pacing around in the back of the classroom. Most were wearing dark sunglasses. They were all taller than I was. I began to get nervous. I saw that my escort was staying in the doorway. As a guard? Maybe that was reassuring?

I would say a few words, start an explanation, and they would interrupt me. Could I get their cousin out on bail? Why did their brother get arrested? I was at a total loss. The class went on that way until the bell rang and it was over.

The escort walked me back. I asked her why the outside door was chained. "To keep the drug dealers out of the school."

"Oh." I asked why I needed an escort.

"Well," she reluctantly explained, "the regular teacher is in the hospital recovering from a stab wound by a student." Great.

I felt obligated to stay the course and to finish my classes. For a completely irrational protection from stabbings I wore an extra layer of a sweater. Just before I finished the course—doubting that the students learned anything and just found me useless to help with their bail questions—a special issue of the Philadelphia city magazine ran a cover story: "Violence in Our Public Schools." My University High School was number one on the list!

I won't mention that I agreed years later to teach "Accounting for Lawyers" at a law school—when I relied completely on the teacher's manual.

I must really like teaching.

chapter ten

ROTARY—HOW #9 LED TO 1, 2, AND 3

EXCUSE US, PLEASE, but we are hoping that you can help us."

Two suited serious businessmen sat across from me at a downtown club, asking a favor. The year was 1989. I was the only senior woman partner in a Minneapolis law firm, with two young children, busy focusing on my billable hours, and I did not know the two men. But I had agreed to meet with them.

Their favor? "Would I please join Rotary?"

"Rotary," I thought, with dismay.

"Please just come visit," they pleaded. "Then you will see what a great group it is."

I did visit, but it just confirmed my reluctance about Rotary. I looked at the sea of all-white, all-middle-aged men, smiling constantly, nodding and clapping, with a big blue flag for Rotary #9 displayed over the podium. Definitely not a place for me. It felt like an alien environment. I didn't need to add another all-male group to my work life.

What was amusing was that they were actually desperate to find some women to be members. I was clearly a prime target. That was a real change from the "boys-only" groups I encountered all too often. I did like being included in general. But Rotary?

I agreed to try it. What was Rotary anyway? I learned a lot about it. It began in 1905 in Chicago with four men who were interested in business networking. Since then it had grown to about 20,000 clubs around the world. At the beginning, a club was named by the number it was in the order of formation. With Minneapolis being fairly close to Chicago, the club I was asked to join was called "Rotary #9" since it was the ninth one to be formed. One of the Rotary expectations was to attend every single week. Club #9 met for lunch on Fridays, not too far from my office. Maybe I could try it.

I knew why they wanted me to join so badly. It wasn't exactly a sudden enlightenment on their part. The U.S. Supreme Court had recently ruled that states could not allow business clubs to refuse to admit women. Rotary #9 finally decided it had better admit some women.

The problem was that they didn't have any lined up to admit. They began a search for "suitable" candidates, and I qualified. I found the whole process somewhat amusing. After my being excluded for so long by so many business associations, I could now do those same men a favor by joining one of their most important clubs. I might as well join and see how it went. I could always quit.

So I began, yet again in the role of a "token woman," but I was surprised to learn that Rotary had some very impressive humanitarian projects. One was to eliminate polio worldwide. They also had numerous exchange programs with other clubs around the world, including a student exchange program.

I had begun to do a lot of international work and liked the idea that as a Rotary member in Minneapolis Club #9, any of the 20,000 other clubs in the world would be required to welcome me to their meetings, even if their club still did not admit women as members. This could be an opportunity for good networking.

I could also use the international visits to maintain my perfect attendance record. Those with perfect (i.e., weekly) attendance were acknowledged—with applause—for their five-year records, ten-year records, and so on. I joined. I got the special Rotary lapel pin and wore it to my Friday lunches and to every foreign club I visited. I got the hang of the attendance rules: you could "make up" for a missed meeting any time within two weeks prior to that meeting or two weeks after that meeting.

It was good that I wore my Rotary lapel pin to other clubs. Outside of the United States I didn't find any clubs at all that had women as members. With my pin, they had to accept me—whether or not they wanted to.

Sometimes I was welcomed, and sometimes I was even flirted with! In Rome an older man in a wheelchair plucked the flowers from his table's centerpiece and wheeled over in front of me to present me with flowers and a kiss on the hand! On the other hand, the local lawyer Rotarian in the Isle of Man warned me: "You can come, but you should know that our club has considered admitting women, and we always vote against it." Welcome to Rotary!

To cement my qualification, and because it just became fun, I started to carry our small Rotary #9 exchange flags as I traveled. At the beginning of each meeting they would ask if there were any visitors. Yes, I was one. I would be asked to come forward for the formal flag exchange: I would give them my flag; they would give me their flag, which I would turn in to my home club where it was added to the large collection.

So I kept up with the visits. Many of the clubs outside of the United States had dinner meetings and included top government officials. Rotary clearly had a very high status. I would look up where the clubs were in the next city I would be in and choose my "make up" visits. I managed to keep this up for ten years of perfect attendance!

The most fun I had in visiting other clubs was to visit clubs in Japan, where I had been going on a regular basis for work. Rotary was extremely popular in Japan. In Tokyo there was a club for each neighborhood. And I was so lucky that my club name was #9 for two reasons. First to be in such an old club was very prestigious to the Japanese. I answered often, "Yes, we were the ninth Rotary Club created in the whole world." Second, the number 9 is a very lucky number in Japan.

The clubs loved getting my #9 little flags. I even learned enough Japanese to introduce myself and my club and thank them for having me. I wore my Rotary lapel pin every day I was in Japan, just in case I spotted another Rotarian. One day the three men across from me on the local subway train saw my pin, came over to talk to me, and invited me to their club. I went.

In Tokyo the men were also fascinated to see a real Rotarian woman. Unlike the Isle of Man, the main Tokyo club had already voted to admit women as members. They just had not been able to convince any women to join. The men would cluster around me at the end of the meeting and ask how they could get women to join. What advice did I have? Could I help them?

Flash forward ten years and many Rotary meetings later. I was trudging along to a Rotary meeting in a classy Tokyo neighborhood—Ebisu. The first challenge, and unfortunately a common one for me in Tokyo, was to figure out exactly where the meeting was and how to get there.

I knew I had to take the subway. I could figure out which line, and saw the stop would be called Ebisu—but I knew that wasn't the end yet. Where exactly was it? It should help that there is usually an enlarged neighborhood map on the wall before exiting the stairs to outside. I had learned the hard way, though, that the map (all in Japanese but with outlines of buildings) probably did not put "north" at the top. It could be positioned in any direction! I got in the habit of carrying a small compass with me on my trips to Japan.

I finally found the Ebisu Rotary Club. When I walked into the meeting, by then a little late, I was eagerly ushered to a table at the front. I looked around and I could hardly believe it. There was a Japanese woman at the podium. She was clearly the president of the club. Absolutely amazing to me. Almost all in the audience were men, and their president was a woman. Most of the reports were in English, maybe for my benefit; I couldn't tell. One report was about the new "Ballroom Dance" committee of the club.

The surprises continued. At the end of the formal meeting, the president put on some music and called everyone to learn how to do the waltz. We all formed in couples and she put the music on. The men stood quietly in pairs.

The president acted as the coach and called out, "One, Two, Three, One, Two, Three" in Japanese. I knew those numbers! My maternal grandmother had given me a monthly series of dolls from around the world. The one from Japan came with a flag and the counting words with a way to remember them: "itchy knee, sun she go." So there I was, with my Rotary lapel pin, in Tokyo, waltzing stiffly with a fellow Rotarian man and hearing the words in my head "itchy knee, sun she go."

I have kept up with that first Rotarian woman president and see her whenever I am in Tokyo. I have known her almost twenty years now. She advanced in Rotary to an international position. Her other activities have included writing a number of books on wealth management, finance for children, and preparedness in life. I would love to read them, but they are only in Japanese. Now she sends me photos of her grandchildren.

I kept going to Rotary after we moved away from Minneapolis, but it wasn't the same. I actually missed being part of the big club #9, complete with all the smiling and clapping. Now, at my encouragement, both of my sisters are members of Rotary, and it continues to do good all over the world.

I always enjoy meeting someone who is wearing the Rotarian lapel pin. I smile, remembering the woman president and her waltz committee in Ebisu, Tokyo. My #9 led me to memories of the 1, 2, and 3 of my childhood.

The Rotary lapel pin

chapter eleven

MY WHITE NIGHTGOWN IS WITH THE MONKS ON MOUNT KOYA

I CAN STILL SEE THE TRAVEL IMMERSION HEATER looped across my hotel bureau handle in Marrakech to cool off. It must be quite cold by now—I forgot to pack it. Darn, I hate losing anything while I travel. I have since bought three or four extra immersion heaters, just in case. They stand ready in my travel accessories drawer at home. Meanwhile, I don't really need one anymore; almost all hotels have coffee ready in the mornings or a hot water heater in the room.

I can list every item I ever lost while traveling. I have a hard time not searching for them, past any reasonable point.

The most extreme search I made to recover a lost item was

for a clever alarm clock I had bought in Tokyo at a gift store connected to the main train station. On my flight back to Minneapolis my overhead bag had an open top, where I had packed the new travel clock. It seemed to have slipped out of the bag during the flight. In any event when I unpacked at home the small clock was missing. It was by Sony, about three inches by two inches, in a silver case.

Yes, I used that description to call the airline I had been on. It was an inexpensive clock, maybe $20, but the point was that I liked it. I filed "missing luggage" claims, talked to "lost and found" and had to accept it was just lost. Well, I didn't quite accept it. I was going to Tokyo again soon . . . and yes I spent half a day there going back to the same shop and thank goodness they still carried the same clock. I gratefully bought it. I still have it, and I have never even used it. But I have it.

Then there was the black cashmere cardigan sweater I bought in Edinburgh when at a conference there. It was perfect. At the airport security line I had to take it off and place it on the conveyor belt. I retrieved my carry-on bags and by the time I reached passport control I realized I didn't have the sweater—I had left it on the belt. I rushed back. Too late. No sweater anywhere. This time my inquiries to lost and found were more perfunctory and without much hope. Today, somewhere someone is wearing a lovely black cashmere sweater from Edinburgh. For myself I bought a similar—never found an identical one—black cashmere sweater that I pack on all trips. I never put it on a conveyor belt.

For a long time I traveled with a favorite nightgown on all my trips. It was white, thin cotton with small buttons all the way down the front. The problem was that it was white. The same color as all the hotel sheets. One day in Texas I came back to the hotel from a client meeting, searched around my pillow area, where I had been keeping the nightgown. No nightgown. How could this happen? I called the hotel service manager and explained that I seemed to be missing a nightgown. They were puzzled, but finally agreed to search their laundry. They found it! It had gotten mixed up with the sheets.

I tried after that to be quite careful checking the whereabouts of my white nightgown. I did not leave it by the pillows; I stuck it in my open suitcase. All was well—until a family vacation in the Netherlands. We spent three weeks going from town to town. All the locals we talked to were amazed that our family of five chose to spend three whole weeks of vacation time in their country. For themselves, they explained, they would go somewhere warm and sunny.

They were right about the weather. Not warm and sunny. I actually had to put my black cashmere sweater on at night on top of my summery white nightgown. Apart from the weather we all had a good time.

Then we arrived in the town of Apeldoorn. I unpacked and no white nightgown. Oh no, how did I miss it again? The night before had been in Kamden. I had their phone number on our hotel bill. So I called, explained, waited for a search by housekeeping—and yes they found it! They were really nice to mail it to me at Apeldoorn. My husband was amused. For all these years later, long after I quit packing a white nightgown, he would check with me before we left a place "did I leave behind any white nightgowns?"

I kept packing that same favorite nightgown for several years. Until Mount Koya, or Koya-san as it is called in Japan, the holy mountain. On that trip, in addition to some client meetings in Tokyo I had two teenage boys with me—to show them Japan. One was our youngest son, who had been on our family trip to

Japan and loved it. The other was a family friend his age who had seldom left Long Island. The three of us spent most of the trip in Tokyo, except for several days when we visited Mount Koya, where I had never been. We could actually stay overnight in a Buddhist monastery. I thought the boys would love it.

As advertised, Koya-san is "one of the best places to experience an overnight stay at a temple lodging where you can get a taste of a monk's lifestyle, eating vegetarian monks' cuisine (*shojin ryori*) and attending the morning prayers." I booked us for overnight in a temple.

Now, how to get there. The website for the excellent Japan train system warns: "In recent years, Mt. Koya has grown to become a top destination for both foreign and Japanese tourists. However, this religious land, hidden away in the mountain, is still difficult to access."

Yes, I would agree; it is difficult to get there. I was determined, so we followed the directions. First a train from Tokyo to Osaka and then, unbelievably, quoting directly from the Japan Rail site:

> The easiest way to get to Gokurakubashi is to take the private line Nankai from Osaka. You can take this line from the Namba or Shin-Imamiya stations, to the terminus Gokurakubashi. Shin-Imamiya Station is accessible by the Osaka Loop Line, there are 5 limited express trains per day that will take you directly to Gokurakubashi for a 1 650 yen fare. It is also possible to take an express or rapid train (departure every 20–30 minutes, 870 yen) that will take you to Hashimoto in less than two hours, from there you will have to take a local train to reach your destination.

> The train station that serves as a gateway to Mount Koya is the Gokurakubashi station on the Nankai line. From this station, the Koyasan (Mount Koya) cable car will take you to the Koyasan stop for 390 yen for a 5-minute journey. Once off the cable car, you will need to take a bus for 10 minutes (290 yen) to Senjuinbashi, the city center where the tourist information office is located.
> In Koyasan itself, it is easy to get around on foot.

I almost felt like giving up, but part of what I love about travel is all the unexpected challenges—and this was clearly a challenge. And we did it! We got there. There were monks wandering around all over with their shaved heads and wearing their scarlet robes. The two teenage boys had to be impressed, though they didn't say anything. Based on our experiences in Tokyo I had the feeling they were quietly looking for a Subway sandwich shop, which they chose gratefully in Tokyo over all local cuisine. I had also learned they needed to eat often.

In Mount Koya—no Subway shops, not even any McDonalds. I loved the forest, the ringing bells and the general quiet. We found our temple and checked in.

We walked around, which was really all there was to do. All our meals were included. Our large room had bamboo mats on the floor and futons to unroll for sleeping. Dinner was brought in for us to eat while sitting on the floor. As each bowl was uncovered, the boys' faces were pictures of dismay. I don't think they ate anything at all for dinner. There was no other food available.

The futons were fine. Breakfast was not—it was even more exotic bowls of mystery foods. The boys didn't eat anything at all for breakfast. Then it was time to begin the journey back to Tokyo.

As I unpacked in Tokyo, I realized I was missing my white nightgown!

This was not a place I could go back to in order to search for the nightgown. This was not even a place I could call to ask for a search. I did try. I asked a friend in Tokyo to compose a polite fax in Japanese asking if they might have found a lady's white nightgown. No reply. Another fax. No reply. So I finally gave up.

Somewhere today in a Mount Koya Buddhist temple is my favorite white nightgown.

I now pack only brightly colored nightgowns.

chapter twelve

"YES, OF COURSE I CAN FIND PINK DIAMONDS"

WELL, WHAT WERE PINK DIAMONDS ANYWAY? Did I even hear her right? I was pretty good at understanding the Saudi accent by then, having been there on a regular basis during the previous ten years.

The woman who asked me about the diamonds was the mother of one of my Saudi clients. She had been so kind to me, inviting me to three weddings, one newborn party, and one graduation party. Each time she went out of her way to explain bits of the Saudi culture. While I rode with her in the back seat of her black limo, she even dabbed my wrists with the special *oud* perfume.

"I have a favor to ask," she said one day.

"Could you find some special pink diamonds?"

I asked her to repeat what she had said. It still sounded like "pink diamonds," and I felt it would be rude to ask her again. I would have to figure it out.

We were visiting in one of the sitting rooms in her home. I remember the conversation well. After she asked if I could find some, she went on to say that she would like some very special ones. They would be a wedding gift for her son to give to his bride.

Those words I understood. In fact, I knew and liked her son very much. How wonderful that he would be getting married. I was already thinking of attending the sure-to-be-lavish wedding. She added that the pink diamonds were to be a surprise. "So don't mention it to my son.

And could I please find some for her.

I might not know pink diamonds, but I did know how to find out about pink diamonds. The value of my having such a great international network meant that I could usually find someone for any purpose.

I remembered that the sister of the wife of a French actor who lived in New York—whom I had met through his mother and her art collection in Brussels—was part of a family that owned an entire building in the diamond district of Manhattan, including a large retail shop. Yes, they would be glad to introduce me to the sister. Yes, she would be glad to meet with me. I went to the retail shop and asked for her. She finished waiting on a customer then came over to me.

As soon as I said "pink diamond," she got very serious and very interested in me!

She led me to a locked display and I asked why they were special. She gave me a detailed lecture on what pink diamonds were and how to judge the value of each one. It was way over my head, but I happily took the explanatory pages and diagrams she offered me. When I mentioned I was looking on behalf of a Saudi client, I felt I had a "new best friend," as they say.

Not only was she more than happy to show me some special pink diamonds—she would even send some to Saudi with me to show the customer if I liked. Wow. I've taken clothes to try on at home before—but I never had someone fly stones, with an escort, from New York to Saudi to show to a customer. How valuable were they anyway?

Starting with color—I learned that pink diamonds are, well yes, pink in color. They could be much more valuable than regular diamonds as they were a lot scarcer. I had the impression we were talking about millions. I was so pleased that my field trip to the diamond district had been a success.

I took the pages and diagrams with me on my next trip to Saudi. I couldn't wait to show the mother what I had found out, including that I now knew an extremely reliable dealer who would charge her a very fair price.

The mother was hard to reach. I got her mobile number from her son, but she was always either gone or didn't answer. I asked the son to let her know I would like to see her. That didn't work either. Darn it, I wasn't able to connect with her the whole trip.

So the next time I went to Saudi I again brought along all my pink diamond papers, reviewing to myself how to explain the diagrams, and I called her again.

Aha, I did reach her. We set a meeting. One of their drivers would pick me up and take me to her home.

This time, for some reason, she also wanted to show me her house. One of the house servants took my *abaya* and we went on a tour. The indoor sunken swimming pool, which we had to walk around, was closed for the winter since the temperature reached as low as 65 degrees outside. The special washing-up gold guest sinks were lined up five in a row for when there were parties. And so on. Everything was gorgeous.

Finally, we were in a sitting room, ready to have our coffee and tea and dates. And I was certainly ready to do my show-and-tell about pink diamonds. I took out my papers and began.

"Oh," she said, "the wedding has been canceled."

I don't know what happened, and I still haven't heard of any new wedding plans.

In any event, it had been fun learning about another luxury item like the pink diamonds. When others became aware of my growing Saudi connections, there were suddenly a lot of unusual requests to me.

"Would I like to see a chess set made of diamonds that might appeal to one of my Saudi clients?" asked an Israeli banker. I turned that one down.

"Could I find a reliable manager based in the Isle of Man for a Saudi private jet?" With my network, that was easy.

"Could I recommend a private security firm for some traveling Saudis in London?" Yes, of course.

A London art curator of a Lebanese art collection asked, "Can you find a painting of a woman with blue colors by a modern well-known artist?"

It turned out that I couldn't, but along the way I learned a lot more.

For that search I started in Zurich, where I had many contacts and where an impressive amount of art is stored in the special tax-free trade zone. One of the lawyers I knew in Zurich referred me to a fascinating pair of women. They had worked together for many years as quiet finders of special art works.

There's a whole network of art dealers that are not visible. The women objected any time I called them dealers. They insisted they themselves were not dealers; they would find dealers, who would then find the art. Often the art would be in a private location, so they would ask the owner if there was any interest in selling.

I described the painting the London curator said her client would like. "No problem" said the two women. "Give us a few days."

They called me a few days later and arranged to take me into the tax-free zone outside of Zurich. After passing through the well-guarded gate, I saw row after row of serious warehouses. The women explained the warehouses were of high quality, well-guarded, and very climate-controlled.

They had made an appointment for us to look at three candidate paintings. The guards opened the first warehouse and brought out a painting that was blue but was of a man with a hoe. Not what I had requested. Neither were the other two. They said they would keep looking, but since I never heard from them again, I assume they never found the perfect woman in blue.

For me, I am ready to tell anyone who asks all I know about pink diamonds, complete with diagrams.

chapter thirteen

MY STREET WITH NINETEEN LETTERS

THE FIRST STREET I KNEW AS MY ADDRESS as a child was the simplest and shortest of all. We lived on Main Street. As I later learned every town in the United States has a Main Street. My parents moved into our simple house on Main Street when I was in the second grade. Before that we had lived in army housing in Pueblo, Colorado. Before that we had lived in Manhattan, in the Upper East Side, where I had been born.

Our small house on Main Street had a box layout: the front had the living room on the right and the kitchen on the left; the back half had two bedrooms and a bathroom. 1030 North Main Street, Carlsbad, New Mexico. I still drive by it when I visit Carlsbad. First it was to show our children, and later to show our grandchildren. A simple house with a simple address.

Then my parents hired an architect and bought some land at the edge of town, across from the river. From my fifth grade of school and for a total of fifty years, the family address was still a short, simple one: Ural Drive.

My addresses after leaving home and getting married varied. In Chicago it was Marine Drive—no longer close to Lake Michigan as I presume it had been when it was named. Then we moved to Philadelphia where we lived on Woodside Avenue, which was in fact wooded. In Washington D.C, it was simply G Street. In Minneapolis our street had a longer name, Humboldt, and later we moved out to Oakview, followed by another stint in Washington D.C., this time on 5th Street, and then ten years on Fifth Avenue in Rochester, Minnesota.

When I had my work apartment in New York, the address was the same as my law firm address had been—the firm had sold the building and it was converted into apartments, at 100 Maiden Lane. So far no street names to get excited about. All were fairly simple and straightforward.

Then in 2007, I got a very appealing offer to work in Zurich. Our children were grown, with families of their own; my husband was busy on the staff at the Mayo Clinic, "so why not?"

I asked what he thought—after all it would be a lot farther away than New York had been. He said, "Why not?"

If it didn't work out, I could always come home.

So I started the process and the paperwork. First I had to get a work permit. These are not so easy to get for Switzerland. I was also warned that I could not go to Switzerland during the work permit process or it might be turned down permanently. The permit finally came.

Then I had to find a place to live and get a residency permit from the city of Zurich. That application asked what religion I was. I asked why they asked and was told that I would owe a tax to that religion. I answered "none."

It turns out that Zurich is one of the most expensive cities in the world and finding housing there is not simple. Anything affordable to rent was on the outskirts of the city, and I wanted to walk to work, which was in the center of the city. I stayed in a low-rent long-term hotel for a few weeks while I searched. It was barely a step up from a college dorm room: one small bed, one chair, and one desk. And I had to take three trams to get to work.

Finally I discovered "serviced" apartments, for people like me who had no furniture and little interest in cleaning. These were almost like a hotel: sheets and towels would be replaced weekly and the apartment would be cleaned weekly. Kitchen appliances were along the wall next to a tiny closet. They were furnished with a clean, modern look. They were very small, but still quite elegant. I chose one.

The address tickled me, and still does. I had gotten used to the German language habit of stringing various descriptive words together to make one word. That had happened in the case of my new serviced apartment: the street name was *Gerechtigkeitsgasse.* Nineteen letters! How did I start out on a simple Main Street and end up on a Gerechtigkeitsgasse?

My two years in Zurich were fascinating and often challenging. To start with, everyone assumed that with my Hauser name, I spoke German, which I don't. I gathered that even traditional German might not be understood well in Zurich, which has its own form of Swiss German.

The ubiquitous greeting was *Guertzi.* Switzerland has three language divisions. The Zurich region is largely German-speaking; the Geneva region is French-speaking; and the Lugano southern region is largely Italian-speaking. I could handle French, and even some Italian—but not German.

I loved telling people the name of my street—even though I had to pronounce it slowly and carefully to get all the syllables in the right order. The apartment was lovely. It was an easy walk to work, passing a well-stocked grocery store, where I finally learned how to weigh my own vegetables. I took many of my evening meals at an Italian restaurant half a block away, where the one waiter who spoke some English was quickly assigned to me. It was a great lifestyle.

There were a few glitches. One was the day I went to a stylish looking beauty shop and asked for "highlights" in my brown hair. She did seem puzzled, and we had almost no language in common. I tried explaining, I pointed to my hair and gestured. Oh yes, she nodded, and I leaned back in the chair. When it was time to take out the wrappers and rinse in the sink she laughed with amusement and announced, "Now you are blond"—and indeed I was.

Across the bridge over the city brook was a large municipal building with an Olympic indoor pool. I had my official city resident permit and managed to buy a pass for the pool. After work it was a decision: Italian restaurant or time in the pool. I did have a TV in my apartment, but I couldn't find any channels in English—not even CNN. When I was at the pool I could also pay to use a weight scale, to keep track of the kilos. They sound so much lighter than pounds.

The trains were marvelous. On weekends I could take a train to all parts of Switzerland. Some of the routes are known as the most splendid train rides in the world. One day I somehow left a new very small and inexpensive computer on the train coming back to Zurich. As soon as I realized it, I asked for the Lost &

Found area. It seemed very Swiss to me when I found it that it was not a Lost & Found bureau; it was simply a "Found" bureau. And my small computer was never found.

The train station itself, with some thirty or forty tracks, contained an entire city underneath it. I bought a lot of my groceries at the Migros shop in the train station, which also had much longer open times than the stores above ground. I used a dry cleaner around the block, on Bleicherweg, and still use one of their Terlinden labeled plastic sheets to pack around my clothes, enjoying the souvenir from my stay in Zurich.

After I had lived on Gerechtigkeitsgasse Street for a year and enjoyed my elegant white apartment, I had dinner in Houston with my Texan sister and one of her good friends. They wanted to hear all about my life in Zurich, so I described the apartment in some detail—adding the name of the street it was on, of course.

My sister is much more into housecleaning than I am. She loves repeating the family story of my four-year-old son visiting our California sister who was vacuuming one day and my son pointed to the machine and asked her, "What is that?"

So at the Houston dinner my Texan sister asked about my cooktop in the fancy apartment—whether it was gas or electric? My pause said it all. I had no idea. I looked when I got back: definitely electric.

After nearly two years, the job was starting to end, and Zurich, as much as I enjoyed my time there, began to seem too far away from my husband to try to keep living in Zurich. So I canceled my Swiss residency and moved back to Minnesota.

I have gone back to Zurich often over the following years, and I always walk over to my old neighborhood and look at the street sign. It's still hard to believe that I once lived on a street with nineteen letters!

Looking ahead, I have applied to the University of Zurich for its Ph.D. program and am waiting to hear of my acceptance. Then I will have to go to Zurich a few more times. And I'll take some more pictures of my favorite street sign, the one that says Gerechtigkeitsgasse. My nineteen-letter street.

chapter fourteen

"YOUR HUSBAND IS IN ZURICH"

"YOUR HUSBAND IS IN ZURICH," announced the Berlin hotel clerk.

Did the hotel clerk get the message right? I was in Berlin. My husband was supposed to be joining me in Berlin.

The annual law conference I was speaking at was in Berlin that year, for a whole week. I had been active in that group—the International Academy of Estate and Trust Law—for some fifteen years. I attended nearly every annual meeting, held in alternating hemispheres, western and eastern. The Academy, as we called it, had a lot of social time built in, and nearly everyone had his (usually the members were men) spouse there also. My husband had never come.

This time, in Berlin, was to be different. Doug had agreed to come. He would come a day or two after it started, but in time to join in the many social evenings. So I had reserved an extra-large hotel room for us both to enjoy.

The room was in a grand old hotel. With a very high ceiling, an elaborate chandelier, and a complex pattern on the faded wallpaper, I anticipated the room would be a real treat for Doug. He was planning to use his airline-parent pass for the trip. We could each fly as parents of our airline son—a perk I used as much as I could.

Doug had never used it, much preferring the certainty of having a ticket over the risky "space available" restriction. Parents were given unclaimed seats, which were allocated at the departure gate moments before the plane's doors closed.

The Academy began with a welcome dinner on Sunday night. I knew Doug would not make that event: he was busy with patients at the Mayo Clinic that Monday. He had told me before I left that he would plan to come on Tuesday, or maybe Wednesday. I told him the name of the hotel in Berlin.

This was before cell phones and before emails. The only way I could hear from him was through the hotel telephone clerk.

Each morning I left the hotel and went to the conference. Each afternoon I came back to the hotel and asked, more and more anxiously, "Do I have any phone messages? Has my husband called?"

Each day it was the same answer—a shrug and "no, *fraulein*." So I would head back to join the Academy group for that evening's parties and dinners.

"Where is your husband, Barbara?" everyone asked.

"He hasn't arrived yet; maybe tomorrow," I answered over and over.

Those were busy years for both of us. I would go to my meetings—clients and conferences—all over the world. Doug had what he and I called a "regular" job, on the medical staff at universities or the Mayo Clinic. He sometimes needed to give as much as three months' notice just to take a day off. I didn't need to give any notice to anyone, so we seldom met anywhere.

This was going to be an exception. It was a fairly small legal group with a heavy schedule of spouse activities. We would have our "academic" sessions in the mornings, from 8 a.m. to noon. The afternoons were filled with a variety of sightseeing activities and the evenings with special dinners and parties.

Only one other lawyer, Michael from Bermuda, never had a spouse along. He and I spent a lot of time together in the social activities each year. He had never met Doug and was looking forward to it. In fact, no one in the group had ever met Doug, so I was being asked each day if he had arrived yet.

"Has Doug arrived yet?"

"No, not yet, but I hope maybe tomorrow."

I knew Doug had left home—there was no answer on the home telephone. But I had no idea where he was. He was not as used to using the last-minute parent-pass on the airline as I was.

I knew it was always a chancy business. I would not know until the last minute if there would be a seat for me on the plane. It was always a gamble. Even when seated on the plane, it was not a sure thing: I had once been asked just before takeoff on one flight to Tokyo if I could gather my belongings and please deplane. So I usually had some alternates in mind. Usually I could get where I wanted eventually.

Doug had given his three months' notice for time off from the Mayo Clinic. On that Tuesday, as planned, he drove from Rochester, Minnesota, up to the Minneapolis airport. He was planning to take the nonstop flight to Frankfurt, then change to Berlin. It looked like an easy trip.

He waited at the gate to be called and given a boarding pass. But the flight to Frankfurt was full, no room for a parent-pass passenger. He had to turn around, get the car, and drive back to Rochester.

In good spirits, he got up the next morning—thinking the day before must have been a fluke—and drove the ninety miles back up to the Minneapolis airport, parked, and went to the gate. He waited patiently, while the plane filled up. No room for a parent-pass passenger. Not quite so happy now, he got the car back from the parking ramp and drove back to Rochester. The next day, Thursday, was going to be his last chance to make it to Berlin in time for the closing gala banquet on Friday. He was quite frustrated by now and knew how much I was looking forward to having him attend the gala banquet.

So this time, back at the Minneapolis airport, he decided he would take any flight to Europe and then see what he could do. He got a seat on a flight to Zurich. He took it.

The Berlin hotel clerk was right. My husband had called. He said he was in Zurich, which is 600 miles from Berlin. That was all I knew.

I got dressed for the gala and paced the floor of my extra-large hotel room. I opened the window and watched the street. Amazed, I saw a taxi open its door and my husband got out! With a quick greeting, I helped him unpack and get out his gala tux. We might just make it.

The group busses had long since left for the gala, but I had the address. We took a taxi and rushed in. They had not yet been seated for the dinner. It was still drinks time. First I found Michael and introduced him to Doug.

Then I circulated as much as possible: "This is my husband."

The reply was usually, "So you do exist!"

The next day he shared the tedious details of why he flew to Zurich, the only flight to Europe with a seat for him and how he then had to buy a one-way last minute ticket to get to Berlin. He never tried using his parent-pass again.

Since Doug had missed all the spouse sightseeing trips and had not seen the new Berlin after the wall was down, we decided to find another hotel to stay in for two more nights in Berlin. We splurged on hiring a private driver the next day to take us from sight to sight. We ended up having a wonderful time together in Berlin. We stopped and got out at Checkpoint Charlie. It wasn't quite what we had planned, but the two days made up for a lot.

About eight years later Doug made it to another of these conferences, this one in nearby Montreal. Everyone greeted him with, "Yes, I remember meeting you in Berlin."

Next year Doug plans to come. It will be in Portugal, a country we like very much. He will ask for the time off at the hospital where he now works. We will both have paid airline tickets.

My colleagues will probably greet him with, "I remember meeting you in Berlin."

chapter fifteen

DO I HAVE COURAGE?

"BARBARA, YOU HAVE SUCH COURAGE!"

I hear that a lot, but it always surprises me. I don't feel like I have unusual courage, so what are they talking about?

"You are so brave, going alone to Saudi Arabia!"

"You have such courage to speak out."

Examples continue—and I've thought about how to explain them. Do I really have unusual "courage"? And if so, when did I first notice it?

I come up with an experience when I was about twelve years old. By then I was a fairly decent horseback rider—Western style—in New Mexico. One day I was out riding with my father and one younger sister, through the cactus-filled lands outside of town.

Suddenly I was thrown off my horse, but not all the way. On the way off, my left boot caught in the stirrup, which left me helpless, my whole body being dragged through the dirt, rough scrubby bushes, and small cactus plants near Carlsbad, New Mexico. Time slowed. Maybe it was just a few seconds, then my boot worked free of the stirrup. My father was with me. I thought he must have been worried too, and I was looking for some sympathy and help, but he shouted, "Get back on." So I did.

I don't know if that was "courage," but that's the earliest example that pops up. I was glad, later, that I did get back on since I kept on riding after that. I even won some blue ribbons at a local rodeo for the barrel races.

When I finished high school I was the only one of my friends who went all the way to the East Coast for college. I took the train alone from Carlsbad to Chicago, changed trains, went on to Boston, and got off at Wellesley. I had never even visited the campus. One reason for my choice was that I thought it was a really pretty name.

I was met at the train station by my assigned "big sister" and given my yellow beanie to wear, for the "sunshine class." Was that courage, to make that trip alone? Yes, I didn't know a soul there and I didn't feel like I fit in with the rest of the girls.

They sounded different than the girls in my high school in New Mexico. They all sounded like each other. They even dressed like each other: prim princess collar ironed cotton blouses, with gold circle pins on the collar, and with matching cardigan sweaters and knee-length skirts. I had brought some ordinary everyday clothes. I would need to go shopping as soon as I could figure out how and where.

I listened to the easy conversations all around me. "Where in France were you this summer?" (I had never been to Europe). "Wasn't the Tanglewood concert delightful?" (What was Tanglewood?)

I heard that it was big news that people like me had even been accepted. "This is the first year we have had more public school girls than private school girls." (Who went to private schools?)

When asked where I was from, they often explained my acceptance into this elite crowd with, "You probably got in because you live in the middle of nowhere."

I stayed at the school and kept trying to fit in. During evenings in the dorm I had no social company. The students were busy studying. In my high school I don't think I ever studied—I wasn't even sure how to do it.

I wandered the halls each night. I was a little surprised not to get all A's. In fact I never got close to getting the grades to be Phi Beta Kappa, which my mother had been at Cornell—not that I'm competitive.

I did enjoy the variety of subjects that were all new to me: Western Civilization, Astronomy, Intellectual History of Russia, Kant, and on and on. Philosophy was my absolute favorite. Reading Plato and Aristotle inspired me to take classical Greek.

I wrote an entire paper on Sartre's *Being and Nothingness* in French. I remember typing in the bathroom on the counter with my typewriter and dictionary on another all-night paper due the next day. I can imagine today how ill-equipped I had been to dare to write in French. I said that of course that was the only way to understand Sartre. But that wasn't courage either—it was a fun experiment.

I also got myself to Europe, with one college friend, to the horror of my parents, who collected news cases of vulnerable college girls being attacked in Europe. Joan and I made our own very serious European tour, guided by the green Michelin 4-star sights and the Frommer travel book *Europe on 5 Dollars a Day*.

We brought our own sewn-together sheet covers, for the

youth hostels, and our own rolls of toilet paper, being warned by Frommer that it would often be missing or of a rough quality. We drove through England, France, Germany, Italy, and Spain in the new VW car that Joan had ordered for us to pick up in Brussels. As we finished a country we tore out that book section and tossed it. We spent one week in each capital, in a budget hotel, and one week in the rest of each country, usually in hostels. But was that courage? I don't think so. It was a great adventure.

After majoring in philosophy, a subject I really did enjoy, my career plan was first to get married (I did, and a premed fellow at that) and then maybe teach part-time, fitting that around a husband, children, and household duties. That was how I was raised—even Wellesley fed us a message (in Latin of course) of "to serve others; not to be served." I almost walked out of the chapel when the college president got to that part.

Going on to graduate school in philosophy clearly didn't take any courage; I coasted into it. Accepted at two programs I chose the one that sounded easier. I had made a mistake on that choice. I found out that the program I had chosen was based on modern "linguistic analysis" with no time for Plato and Aristotle or even Kant. Still I looked at the other students and thought, "I will pass if anyone does." No one did.

Married then—right after college graduation—I needed to move with my husband to his posting on the Navajo Indian Reservation. I was a long way from the philosophy graduate program in Chicago. I did manage to be the last student to not complete the program.

What to do next? Our first child was already born, on the reservation, but I had learned that I needed some kind of future career path. I had grown up knowing only doctors and lawyers. I didn't enjoy seeing sick people or my volunteer work as a Candy

Striper at the hospital where my father worked. No one in the family had been a lawyer. I wasn't too sure what lawyers did. Given the two choices—I thought I might apply to law school.

First I would give philosophy another try to. I knew we were moving next to Philadelphia for Doug's next step in his medical training, so I applied to teach philosophy at every college I could find within range of Philadelphia. I got all negative replies—except one from Glassboro State College looking for a tenured position for someone who had already published in Far Eastern religions. I applied.

The man who interviewed me was puzzled but polite. He suggested that I start by teaching one simple course on a basic introduction to Far Eastern religions. That was fine with me since I knew nothing at all about Far Eastern religions. Did that take courage? I don't think so. It wasn't that hard to find some good books on the subject and to "read, then teach."

Next was law school. I can't say that took courage because I enjoyed it so much. I even enjoyed law review, with those hours spent proofreading. After law school I spent two years with appellate clerkships—also fascinating and "fun." Did it take courage to be the first pregnant clerk in the history of the Supreme Court? It didn't seem like it at the time. If anyone acted surprised that I was looking more and more pregnant, they were polite enough not to mention it. I was amused to think that not only was I pregnant I also had two small children at home. I am pretty sure there had never been a mother as a clerk.

Joining a law firm and working my way up to a corner office—yes, there was a lot of courage along the way. At that time law firms were not sure how to handle female lawyers. We were not so sure ourselves. I studied *Dress for Success* and even had a men's tailor shop make two three-piece suits for me, with skirts and pants both. I wore the popular floppy scarf necktie. I displayed no family photos—especially not of children. I made it to the corner office. Tenacity more than courage?

After reaching that goal, did it take courage to leave it? When the headhunter called me, looking for someone like me to give full-time advice to a billionaire, it was not hard to say "yes." It sounded like another fascinating adventure. And it was, and it lasted for four years. To everyone else, it seemed to look like courage.

What next? I did some teaching at a law school, did some consulting, worked briefly for a global bank, tried working in Switzerland for two years, did a stint in a Paris *notaire*'s office, did one in a Tokyo law firm, wrote a treatise on international estate planning, wrote a book of travel stories, and finally chose to be truly independent, without staff or office.

My main client base turned out to be Saudi family businesses. When I started going to Saudi Arabia on a regular basis, by myself, to give advice to Saudi patriarchs on how to keep their families (and businesses) together—well, everyone I knew called that courage, or foolish!

Thinking about the word "courage" now, I think the reason it never seemed quite the right word because it wasn't action of the "daredevil" type. I simply liked having adventures.

What do we mean by "courage" anyway? The Greek philosopher Thucydides has this insight: "The secret to happiness is freedom . . . And the secret to freedom is courage." That's a start.

Then we have Confucius: "Wisdom, compassion, and courage are the three universally recognized moral qualities of men."

With my love of travel and fierce independence, maybe it's courage that supports the willingness—actually more like eagerness—to go on adventures. But it doesn't feel reckless at all. And it isn't being fearless. I know that. I was afraid to take pilot lessons, or do a parachute jump, or do a second nighttime scuba dive, or board a small plane in a Colorado blizzard. In other words, I have had cautionary times too.

Back to Saudi Arabia. I've gone there, alone, some fifty times. That alone sounds like courage. Lots of questions, from everyone.

"Barbara, do you have to wear a *burka*?"

"Actually in Saudi it is called an *abaya*, and yes I wear one and a headscarf—both black—or else go to jail. It isn't very different from wearing black clothes in Manhattan. The zipper front reminds me of my Presbyterian church choir robe.

My mother hates the idea though, says I am above that, and a more independent woman, and so on.

So no courage needed based on what I wear in Saudi.

"Barbara, the region is having revolutions. It's the Arab Spring. You should not go, please."

This from my husband, and every one of our three sons, who don't usually offer advice about my travel plans. Yes it was the Arab Spring with revolutions and protests throughout the Gulf Region, but Saudi looked held together by threats ("prohibits revolts" and "outside agitators will have their hands chopped off") and treats (immediate work bonuses, more money for the religious police, immediate time off). Should I go?

I called Emirates Air. I called Saudia Air. I called friends at the U.S. embassy in Riyadh. Everyone said all is fine. Not so the media. There were curfews, cancelled flights, and armed tanks crossing the bridge from Saudi to Bahrain. I couldn't decide whether to go or not.

At the time I was in London, staying in the home of French friends. Gigi had grown up living through the revolution in Algeria. She had wise, practical advice.

"Barbara," she said very seriously, "go, but the minute you feel uneasy, take the first plane out, to anywhere."

Whew, I had a plan. I went. Maybe this was courage, mixed with adventure. I should mention Pakistan. I did go to Lahore twice to meet with a Pakistani family. The second time I went it was a few days after the U.S. had killed Osama bin Laden, in that neighborhood. All the other Americans were leaving in their armored cars. I was arriving.

I'll end with a different example, one that makes me laugh every time I think of it.

I was in Paris, strolling through the Luxembourg Gardens, on the Left Bank, with Jeannette, a Parisian I had recently met. The day was postcard perfect: spring flowers, blue sky, dry paths, and classic statues scattered around.

We were speaking in careful English, through her French lens, which I was usually able to understand. For example I love how the French use hyperbole more than we do in the Midwest. "No, I am desolate that I do not have an umbrella for you," the hotel manager will say.

We had walked for twenty minutes through the lovely gardens when Jeannette stopped, turned to me, and asked, "Do you have the courage to continue walking?"

Yes, I did have the courage.

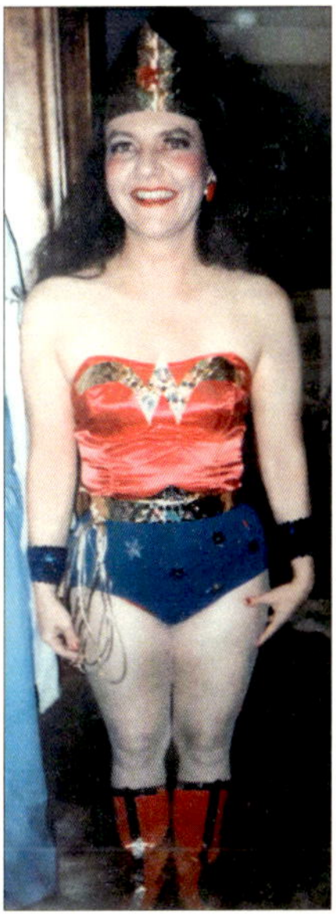

In my era career women with children were called "wonder woman."

The real voyage of discovery
consists not in seeking new
landscapes but in having new eyes.

Marcel Proust